EXAMINING
RELIGIONS

Christianity

Joe Jenkins

HEINEMANN
EDUCATIONAL

Heinemann Educational,
a division of Heinemann Educational Books Ltd,
Halley Court, Jordan Hill, Oxford OX2 8EJ

OXFORD LONDON EDINBURGH
MADRID ATHENS BOLOGNA PARIS
MELBOURNE SYDNEY AUCKLAND SINGAPORE
TOKYO IBADAN NAIROBI HARARE GABORONE
PORTSMOUTH NH (USA)

First published 1989
91 92 93 94 95 13 12 11 10 9 8 7 6 5 4

British Library Cataloguing in Publication Data
Jenkins, Joe
Christianity.
1. Christianity
I. Title II. Series
200

ISBN 0 435 30312 0

Designed and produced by Gecko Limited, Bicester, Oxon
Printed and bound in Great Britain by Butler & Tanner
Ltd, Frome and London

Acknowledgements

The author would like to thank the following people for
guidance in the writing of this book:
Brother Robert and the Brothers of Belmont Abbey,
Hereford; Philippa Bowley; Owen Cole; Paula Cook; Ann
Hammond; Trevor Huddleston; Fred Hughes and the
College of St Paul and St Mary, Cheltenham; Ellen
Jenkins; John St John; Satish Kumar; Robert Cameron
Mitchell; Howie Phillips; Reverend Richard Roberts;
Dorothy Rowe; Dave Sharp; Jenny Taylor; Bronwen
Turner; Joan Turner; Steve Turner and Beat the Border;
Sue Walton; Cordelia Weedon; Mike Williams.

Thanks are due to Religious Studies Consultant W. Owen
Cole, Sister Ruth Duckworth, Roger Owen and Arye
Forta for commenting on the manuscript.

Thanks are also due to the following for permission to
reproduce copyright material: Advent for the extracts
from the *Additional Curates Society Magazine* on pp. 103
and 104; Allen and Unwin Australia for the extract from
Contemplation in a World of Action on p. 42; BBC for the
extract from the *Scene* programme for schools on p. 65;
Beat the Border for the logo on p. 137; Ian Bradley for the
article on p. 153; Brother David for the article on p. 43;
Catholic Institute for International Relations for the
extract from *The Kairos Document* on pp. 132–3; Catholic
Truth Society for the poster on p. 9, the Roman Catholic
Catechism extract on p. 32, the table on p. 44 and the
extract from *Human Work* on p. 116; Christian Aid for the
Christmas Appeal advertisement on p. 83; Christian
Education Movement for the two extracts from *The
Ecumenical Movement* on pp. 58 and 59; Church of England
Board for Social Responsibility for the extract from *The
Church of England and Racism – And beyond* on p. 128;
Church of Wales Publications for the canticle on p. 53; T
and T Clark for the extract from *The Church and Racism
(Concilium no. 151)* on p. 29; William Collins Sons & Co
Ltd for the extracts from *Hymn of the Universe* on pp. 27
and 97, for the extracts from *Christianity and World
Religions* on pp. 31 and 59, for the extracts from *Hope and
Suffering* on pp. 70 and 131 and for the extracts from
Nought for Your Comfort on p. 130; Darton, Longman &
Todd Ltd for the extract from *Contemplative Prayer* on
p. 41; J M Dent and Sons Ltd for the poem from *The Poems*
on p. 89; Eyre and Spottiswoode Ltd for the extracts from

the *Alternative Services Book* on pp. 77 and 98; Faber and
Faber Ltd for the extract from *The Last Temptation* on p. 33;
Hodder and Stoughton for the extract from *Fear No Evil* on
p. 25, the extract from *The Social Hope of the Church* on
p. 96, and for the extract from *Nuclear Holocaust and
Christian Hope* on p. 146; *The Independent* for the article on
p. 113; The Estate of Martin Luther King for the extracts
from *The Trumpet of Conscience* on pp. 36 and 81; Leeds
City Council for the extract from *Leeds and the Bomb* on
p. 146; Lion Publishing for the quote from the *Lion Concise
Book of Christian Thought* on p. 47 and for the extract from
the *World Christian Encyclopedia* on p. 56; Methuen and Co
Ltd for the extract from *Churchmen and the Condition of
England* on p. 112; *New Internationalist* for the quote on
p. 140 and for the articles on pp. 55, 141 and 150; Nisbet
for the quote from *The Nature and Destiny of Man* on p. 88;
Orthodox News for the adapted extract on p. 48; Penguin
Books Ltd for the poem on p. 71 and the extract from
Revolutionary Priest on p. 140; Pergamon Press for the
extracts from *Religion and Social Justice* on pp. 36, 110, 120
and for the extract from *Christian Denominations* on p. 100;
Simon Phipps for the extract on p. 149; Picador for the
quote from *If the War Goes On* on p. 31; Edward Pilkington
for the article on p. 114; Religious Experience Research
Unit for the extract from *The Divine Flame* on p. 103;
Resurgence for the extracts on pp. 108–109 and 149; Jan
Rocha for the article on p. 151; Routledge and Kegan Paul
for the extracts from *Living with the Bomb* on pp. 146 and
147; Alan Rusbridger for the article on p. 65; Sheldon
Press for the extract from *The Social God* on p. 112; Tabor
Publishing 25115 Ave. Stanford, Valencia, CA 91355 for
the extract from *African Primal Religions* in the series *Major
World Religions* on p. 57; *The Universe* for the article on
p. 91; Jean Vanier for the article on p. 66–67; WCC
Magazine for the extract on p. 60.

Acknowledgements are due to the following for
permission to reproduce photographs: Agence France
Press p. 112; Amnesty International p. 134; Andes Press
Agency pp. 14 (top), 38 (top and bottom right), 94 (top
left, centre left and bottom); Deirdre Mckenna/L'Arche p.
67; BBC Hulton p. 61; Hilda Bernstein p. 32; Vanden
Bossche p. 148; Malcolm Brenner p. 152; Camera Press pp.
6, 17, 24, 37, 38 (centre and bottom left), 74 (right);
William Campbell/*Time Magazine* p. 9; J. Allan Cash pp.
34, 49 (left); Keith Ellis Collection pp. 50, 86, 94 (centre
right) 98, 121; Rex Features pp. 58, 63, 106, 145; Findhorn
Foundation p. 42; Format pp. 84 (Brenda Prince), 101 (Val
Wilmer), 129 (Val Wilmer), 142 (Jenny Matthews); Armet
Francis p. 56; Glasgow Art Gallery and Museum p. 87;
Gloucestershire Echo p. 137; Sally and Richard Greenhill pp.
72, 124, 127; *The Guardian* p. 64; Hutchison pp. 20, 76, 90,
94 (top right), 151; IDAF p. 130; *The Independent* p. 116;
International Defence and Aid Fund p. 110; Robin
Kennedy p. 136; Susan Meiselas p. 143; NASA p. 26;
Stephen Dalton/NHPA p. 92; NSPCC p.118; National
Gallery pp. 8, 10; National Trust for Scotland p. 12;
Network/Mike Abrahams p. 69; Orthodox News p. 80;
Palomar Observatory p. 5; Phaidon Press p. 88;
Popperfoto pp. 22, 28, 44, 46, 132, 147; Carlos Reyes/
Andes Press Agency pp. 79, 93, 94 (top left, centre left and
bottom), 96, 104, 122; Riverman Designs p. 30; Shelter/
Andrew North p. 115; Society for Cultural Relations with
the USSR p. 105; Homer Sykes p. 54; Tropix Photo Library
pp. 14 (bottom), 138; United Society for the Propagation
of the Gospel p. 79; Simon Warner p. 73; Cordelia
Weedon pp. 18, 108; Whitworth Art Gallery p. 21;
Woodmansterne p. 52; World Council of Churches pp. 70,
102.

Cover photographs by: Carlos Reyes/Andes Press Agency
(people singing and taking of communion); Hutchison
Library (stained glass window).

CONTENTS

1 INTRODUCTION

We live in an unimaginably huge universe. I find myself in this place at this particular time. How did the earth and the universe come into being? Who am I? What is my life all about? Why am I here? Where am I going? Is there any purpose or meaning to life? It is part of being human to ask questions about our existence. Human beings have always asked questions about the universe, about the world and about themselves. Throughout human history there have appeared great teachers who have helped people to try and answer these and other questions about life. These teachers have included Abraham, Moses, Confucius, Lao–Tzu, the Buddha, Jesus Christ, Muhammad, Guru Nanak and many others. From theirs and other teachings the great religions of the world have developed – Judaism, Confucianism, Taosim, Buddhism, Christianity, Islam, Sikhism and Hinduism. These teachings and religions have inspired countless people to find meaning and purpose in their lives and continue to do so today.

From the dawn of human history women and men have felt and have believed that the world that we can see, hear, taste, touch and experience is not the only reality. People have believed, and continue to believe, that as well as the visible world – the physical, external world – there is a deeper, hidden world that we can't see. That is the internal, invisible world – the spiritual world. Above, beyond and within the sights and sounds of this world, there lies another reality. This other reality is the spiritual world.

The search

The modern western world has often been called 'secular'. This basically means that this part of the world is no longer 'religious'. However, on a deeper level, because we are human we still ask basic questions about our existence. We are all still searching for meaning in our lives. Whatever happens to the outer (external) world we still feel a deep need to explore and understand our inner (internal) world. The questions that religions ask, and the answers they try to give, help people to explore and understand the external and internal worlds.

This book

This book has been written to help you understand one of these great religions, namely the Christian religion. Every part of the world has been influenced by various religions and spiritual beliefs. In certain parts of the world, including our own, Christianity has had and continues to have a major influence on the way we think, on our history and on our culture.

This book does not suggest in any way that Christianity is the only religion that matters. Of course, for millions of people both here and abroad the Christian faith is of great importance. In the same way, for millions of people both here and abroad, some of the other great religions are of profound importance.

In the past, Christianity was influenced by the religion of Judaism. At present, for example in Africa, it is influenced by African tribal religions. In Britain today there are many people who follow other religions, helping to create what is known as a 'multi-faith' society. This results in a rich and diverse society, with a variety of music, literature, food, dress, beliefs, customs and so on.

Often, when people don't understand something, they tend to 'stereotype' it. This means they fix an idea of something or someone into a mould which they are not prepared to change. They then insist that this mould is the only possible one. People often stereotype religions as well as stereotyping the followers of religions.

This book aims to begin to break down some of these stereotypes. Stereotyping can lead to dangerous prejudices. It is usually the result of ignorance. If we don't know about something, we tend to stereotype it, and then pretend that we do know. However, each human life is too precious, too mysterious and too important to be stereotyped, and the same is also true of religions.

Because religions are concerned with the external and internal aspects of life they tend to raise many questions about our own existence. This book aims to make you think for yourself about your own life and your relationship to the world. It aims to make you ask some questions about life. The book does not intend to force any particular beliefs or views on you. It is designed to help you to understand Christian beliefs about life and how these beliefs affect people's lives, and also to help you to think for yourself.

How to use this book

The book is divided into five broad themes: Jesus and the birth of the Church, Christian beliefs, The Christian Church, Worship, and Christianity in the modern world.

Each self-contained unit contains a wide range of tasks – written work for your folders, discussion topics and talking points. Each unit gives relevant information, helps you to understand the main ideas and makes you think for yourself about these ideas. These three areas are very important and relate to the skills you will develop in Religious Studies:

1 obtain, organize and clearly present information;
2 show that you understand the information;
3 evaluate – which means being able to give both sides of an argument and to give your own ideas, using sound judgement and good reasons. When you see this symbol ! then you will be expected to give your own views and use good reasons.

Throughout history people have believed that as well as the external world (p.115) there is an internal, invisible world

2 JESUS OF NAZARETH

Palestine is still a land racked with problems

The life of Jesus is recorded in the Christian **Bible** in the first four books of the New Testament. These are called the Gospels, a Greek word meaning 'good news' (see unit 6). These books, the Gospels of Matthew, Mark, Luke and John, were written at different times by different people between thirty and seventy years after Jesus' death. Apart from the four Gospels there is also other ancient literature that mentions the man called Jesus. Although some people have tried to argue that Jesus never really existed, all the literature that has been written about him suggests that such a person did exist.

However, the question 'Who was Jesus?' has caused much debate over the centuries and still continues to do so today. Some Christians believe that every claim made about Jesus, and every story about him as recorded in the New Testament, is absolutely accurate. Others believe that these claims and stories are open to different interpretations. However, for all Christians, the story of Jesus plays a central role in Christian belief and practice. For most Christians, Jesus is not only an important historical figure – he is a living person who shares in their daily lives.

Background

Jesus was a Palestinian Jew. As it is today, Palestine (now called Israel) was a land racked with problems, conflicts and violence. Jesus was born around 4 BCE into an ordinary working-class family. As a young man he made a name for himself as a religious teacher. He was in the public gaze for only about three years and little is known about his life between the ages of twelve and thirty. When he was about thirty-three his life was brutally ended when he was executed by the Romans, who occupied Palestine at the time. However, during his three years of teaching, preaching, healing and travelling around the country he delivered a message that was to have a massive impact on the subsequent course of human history.

Jesus' appearance in Palestine at that time was not really out of the ordinary. The Jewish religion had many hundreds of travelling 'rabbis' (teachers) who possessed great wisdom and who attracted followers. The stories in the New Testament tell how Jesus had twelve followers (called **disciples** or **apostles**) and how he often attracted large crowds to hear his teachings. However, his teachings did not always please the authorities in Palestine, nor did his life style, since he kept company with people who were often regarded as social outcasts. He was arrested in Jerusalem, tried and then crucified.

However, for his disciples or followers (and for Christians today) the story didn't end there. They claimed that Jesus rose from the dead after three days. This became known as the Resurrection. Less than twenty years afterwards every major civilization round the Mediterranean Sea contained at least one group of his followers.

Profile

It is only possible to give the briefest sketch of Jesus' life here. Read the biblical references to get more background.

HIS BIRTH

The stories in Matthew's and Luke's Gospels tell how God's Spirit mysteriously entered a young girl called Mary. She was to have a baby son and was to call him 'Jesus', a Hebrew name meaning 'God saves' or 'Saviour'. For many years the Jewish people had been looking forward to the coming of a 'Messiah'. The word 'Messiah' means 'anointed one' or 'Christ', and at the time such a person was expected to overthrow Roman rule in Palestine and restore the Jewish state of Israel to its former greatness.

HIS WORK

The Gospels are full of stories about how Jesus was able to heal the sick and how he had great power over nature. He is also spoken of as being a great teacher who used simple stories to explain his message. His teachings often had a deep inner meaning about life and God, and they still inspire Christians today. Sometimes his teachings challenged or questioned the ideas and practices of his day. Often he was in conflict over his teachings and his life style with the religious leaders of his day.

THE PASSION

This refers to the last week of Jesus' life and his death on the cross. Accounts of the Passion can be found in all four Gospels.

THE RESURRECTION

All the Gospels record the appearance of Jesus to his followers after his death.

BIBLICAL REFERENCES

Matthew 5, 6 and 7 (*The Sermon on the Mount*)
Mark 2 (*Jesus beginning his ministry*)
Luke 15 (*Three parables*: simple stories with deep meanings)
John 18, 19 and 20 (*The Passion*)
Matthew 28 and Luke 24 (*The Resurrection*)

FOR YOUR FOLDERS

▶ Explain the following words: Gospels; rabbi; disciples; Messiah.
▶ After reading this unit and looking up the references make a profile of the life of Jesus.

Born in poverty. Lived only 33 years. Spent most of his life in obscurity. Never wrote a book. Never had any position in public life. Was crucified with two thieves, **and yet** 2,000 years later, more than 950 million people follow him.

3 CLAIMS ABOUT JESUS

'I believe in . . . one Lord Jesus Christ, the only begotten Son of God, begotten of his Father before all worlds, God of God, Light of Light, very God of very God, begotten not made, being of one substance with the Father; by whom all things were made; who for us men and for our salvation came down from heaven, and was incarnate by the Holy Ghost of the Virgin Mary, and was made man . . .

(Nicene Creed, fourth century CE)

At the very centre of Christian faith are beliefs about Jesus Christ. In this part of the fourth-century Nicene Creed, an early Christian statement of belief, we can begin to understand some of the claims made by Christians about Jesus and the beliefs they hold about him.

- Jesus is the *only* Son of God; he is unique.
- Jesus Christ existed before anything else, because he is 'one substance' with (the same as) God. He and God ('the Father') existed together. Jesus was not made.
- Jesus is God.
- Jesus came down to earth to save people.
- Jesus was **incarnate**. This means he became flesh and blood and took on human form. God became a human being and so Jesus is both human and 'God-like' (divine). God was born in Jesus, lived on earth, died, then rose from the dead.
- Christians believe not only that Christ was God, but also that God is a **Trinity** (in three parts) – the Father, the Son and the Holy Spirit. The idea of the Trinity is difficult to understand and is regarded by Christians as being a great mystery. How can three be one? Indeed some Christians often emphasize one of the three more than the others. However, traditionally, the Church has said:

  'We worship one God in Trinity and Trinity in Unity . . . none is greater or lesser than the other . . . the Unity in Trinity and Trinity in Unity is to be worshipped.'

  (Athanasian Creed, sixth century CE)

In paintings through the ages (see opposite) artists have tried to illustrate the idea of the Trinity.

Christians believe in the idea of **atonement** (making amends for past wrongs) by which Jesus saved the world from its sins. They believe that Jesus did this in the following ways:

- Jesus was a sacrifice. By dying Jesus 'brought back' people from evil, which had taken control of the world when the first man Adam had disobeyed God (see Genesis 3).

An artist's view of the Trinity

- People die because they are sinful. However, because Jesus had no sin, his death 'atoned' for (paid off) all the sins of the world and gave back to people the possibility of returning to God forever.

KEY WORDS

Incarnation – the idea that God became fully human.
Trinity – the idea that there are three persons (the Father, the Son and the Holy Spirit) in one.
Atonement – the idea that Jesus' life and death saved the world from its sins.

FOR YOUR FOLDERS

▶ The three key words refer to quite difficult ideas. After reading this unit try to illustrate with three pictures what these ideas are.

▶ After reading this unit write a letter to somebody who knows nothing about Christian claims about Jesus, explaining to them what these claims are.

! ▶ What are your views on these various claims made about Jesus? Give reasons for your views.

An African image of Christ

4 CHRISTIANITY – THE EARLY YEARS

An artist's impression of the Pentecost

The fifth book in the New Testament is called the Acts of the Apostles, and was written during the latter part of the first century CE by a disciple of Jesus called Luke. His book is the chief source of information about the beginnings of the Christian Church. The following passage is taken from Acts 2 and is an account of what happened to Jesus' disciples during the Jewish festival of Pentecost, fifty days after Jesus' death:

'When Pentecost day came round, they had all met in one room, when suddenly they heard what sounded like a powerful wind from heaven, the noise of which filled the entire house in which they were sitting; and something appeared to them that seemed like tongues of fire . . . they were all filled with the Holy Spirit, and began to speak foreign languages as the Spirit gave them the gift of speech.'

(Acts 2:1–4)

Christians do not agree on the exact meaning of Luke's story. Some believe that the events did really happen as described, that is, that the disciples actually heard the sound of a great wind and saw tongues of fire in the air. Other Christians think that Luke used wind and fire as symbols of the power and excitement with which the disciples were inspired. However, Luke's message is that the first Christians believed that in founding their Church they were acting under God's inspiration. Luke says that on the morning of Pentecost there were about 120 disciples of Jesus in Jersualem, but by evening their numbers had increased to over 3000. Luke's message is clear – only fifty days after the death of Jesus, his message could inspire large numbers of people to be his disciples and from that time on the new religion of Christianity was a force to be reckoned with in the ancient world.

During the first two centuries CE the Christian religion began to spread across the known world. Two of the most important figures during this period were Peter, a disciple of Jesus, and Saul of Tarsus, a Jew who later called himself Paul.

Jesus had said to Peter:

'You are Peter, the Rock; and on this rock I will build my church.'

(Matthew 16:18)

These words prove to some Christians that Peter was meant to be the leader of the early Church. This passage in Matthew's Gospel is especially important to Roman Catholic Christians, the largest group of Christians, who regard their leader, called the Pope, as being the successor of Peter (see unit 21).

As the Christian religion began to spread, opposition to it grew and many Christians were killed by its opponents. One such opponent, Saul of Tarsus, took part in this 'persecution' (inflicting suffering on others). However, one day he experienced an event that changed his life. Whilst walking on a road he was blinded by a vision and he heard a voice say, 'Saul, Saul, why do you persecute me?' After this he became convinced of the truth of the Christian faith and set out on long journeys all over the ancient world telling people about Christianity. On his journeys Paul wrote many letters, called Epistles, which are to be found in the New Testament. In the Epistles, Paul does not recount the life of Jesus, but tries to explain what the early Christians felt was the enormous significance of Jesus' life for the world. After many adventures he arrived in Rome, the capital city of the ancient world, and was beheaded by the Romans. They believed that their emperor was God, not some Jewish teacher whom they had crucified decades ago.

In the early years Christians met in houses or in the open air to worship. There were no actual churches built for the first 300 years due to the persecution and poverty of Christians. During this period the Christians thought that Jesus would come again and that the end of the world was very near, so there seemed little point in building places of worship. However, as the years passed, leaders of the Church, called bishops, were appointed to look after the areas where there were large groups of Christians.

It was not until the third century CE that the Roman emperors began to tolerate Christianity. The Emperor himself, called Constantine, became a Christian and built a new city called Constantinople. Churches were built and the Christian religion became the new religion of the Roman Empire.

FOR YOUR FOLDERS

▶ Why do you think that Christians regard Pentecost as being the 'birthday of the Church'?

▶ Why do you think that the early Christians were persecuted? Can you think of groups of people who are persecuted in the world today?

▶ Read Acts 27. In this chapter we can begin to get an idea of the adventures and difficulties Paul experienced during his journeys. Why do you think the Christian Church regards Paul's journeys as being very important in the history of Christianity?

5 LANDMARKS IN CHRISTIAN HISTORY

325 CE The Council of Nicaea

Arguments about who Jesus was began very early in the history of Christianity. The study of religion is called '**theology**', and Christian theologians soon began to disagree about certain '**doctrines**' (teachings). Questions like: 'Is Jesus truly God?' 'Was Jesus merely a man?' 'Is he both?' were discussed. The first Christian emperor, Constantine, called together the first **ecumenical** (world-wide) council of the Christian Church in Nicaea, to discuss these and other questions. The assembled bishops issued a statement about Christian belief (called a **creed**): the Nicene Creed. However, the debates and discussions continued.

c. 530 CE The first monastery

In Monte Cassino in Italy, an Italian Christian called Benedict formed a community of men who totally dedicated themselves and their lives to God. Benedict wrote a list of rules by which all his monks had to live (see unit 19).

563 CE Columba

A Celtic monk, Columba, started a monastery on the Isle of Iona off the west coast of Scotland. Iona became a centre for the spread of Christianity throughout Britain (see unit 29).

1054 CE The Great Schism

The word 'schism' means 'tear' in Greek. Over the centuries two main centres of power had developed within Christianity. One was in Rome and the other in Constantinople. After much argument between the Pope (the head of the Church in Rome) and the Patriarch (the head of the Church in Constantinople), the two centres were torn apart and separated. From this time on, there were two great Christian Churches in the world: the '**Catholic**' (universal) Church which is based in Rome; and the '**Orthodox**' (right-thinking) Church which is based in Constantinople.

1233 CE The Inquisition

The history of Christianity has often been marred by terrible brutality and bloodshed. Pope Gregory IX set up an **Inquisition** (a tribunal or court) to search out and destroy people who were regarded as being 'heretics' (people who did not follow the teachings of the Roman Catholic Church). The Inquisition was cruel, violent and terrifying. Christain theologians went to great lengths to justify using terrible methods of torture to force confessions from so-called heretics. They said it was better for a heretic to suffer pain on earth rather than suffer eternal torture in hell. People found guilty of heresy were handed over to the state and burnt at the stake.

Iona became a centre for the spread of Christianity

1517 CE The Reformation

During the Middle Ages the Church had enormous power. Many people began to think that the Church was abusing this power. In 1517 a German priest called Martin Luther nailed a document on a church door condemning many of the practices of the Church. This was the start of a wave of Church reform which swept through Germany. Many people believed, like Luther, that the Church had lost sight of the true message of Jesus and had become too concerned with wealth and the material world. Luther's act was the beginning of a widespread movement which split the western world. His protest marked the beginning of the formation of the Protestant Churches which began to pull away from the power of Rome.

1534 CE King Henry VIII became supreme Head of the Church in England

King Henry VIII and Pope Leo X came into dispute because the Pope refused to let the King have a divorce. Henry declared himself Head of the Church in England to replace the Pope. After Henry's death, this break with Rome heralded the Reformation in England.

1545 CE The Council of Trent

The Roman Catholic Church formulated doctrines to protect itself against the growing Reformation. For a hundred years Europe was torn by wars and persecution which often had religious causes.

1859 CE The Origin of Species by Charles Darwin published

In this book Darwin argued that many different forms, or species, of life on earth had undergone great changes over millions of years in a process called 'evolution'. Many Christians saw this as a direct attack on the Biblical view of creation as outlined in the book of Genesis. Modern science seemed to be contradicting the long-held view amongst Christians that the world had been created over a short space of time by God. The great debate between science and religion still continues today.

1948 CE The World of Churches (WCC) formed

Many different churches, after many years of serious disagreements, decided to meet and work for greater unity within the Christian religion. This working towards unity has become a very important part of Christianity in the latter part of the twentieth century (see unit 28).

1962 CE The Second Vatican Council

This was one of the most important meetings of Roman Catholics in the history of the Catholic Church. The Council worked to bring the Roman Catholic Church into the modern world on all sorts of issues and doctrines (see unit 22).

KEY WORDS

theology	Catholic
doctrines	Orthodox
ecumenical	Inquisition
creed	Reformation
Great Schism	

FOR YOUR FOLDERS

► After reading this unit write a sentence about the above key words and phrases.

► Write a brief profile on the following important figures: Constantine; Benedict; Columba; Pope Gregory IX; Martin Luther; King Henry VIII; Charles Darwin.

► 'The history of Christianity has been one of change and conflict.' Explain, with examples, what you think this statement means.

A lectionary gives readings for each week

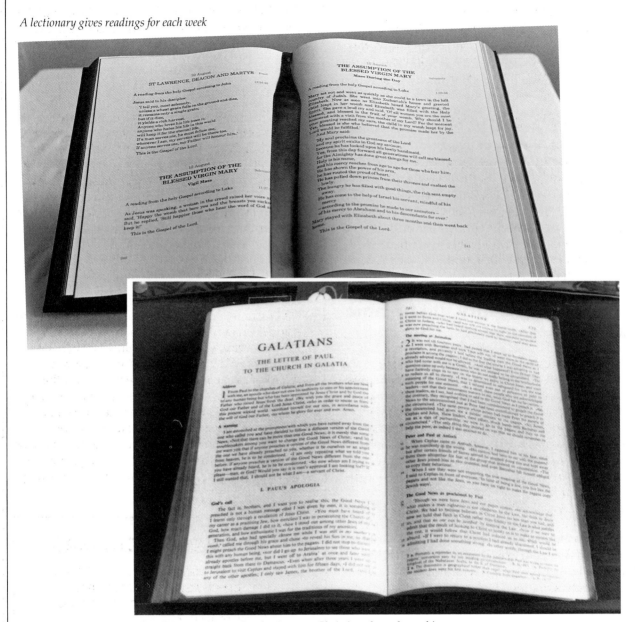

The Bible is read every Sunday in every Christian place of worship

The **Bible** is the holy book of Christians. The word 'Bible' comes from a Greek word which means 'the books'. The Bible is not really one book; it is more like a library.

A library

Christians have often disagreed about how many books there are in the Bible. All accept, as part of the Bible, the thirty-nine books of the Jewish scriptures and these are known to Christians as the Old Testament. The Old Testament was written mainly in Hebrew and consists of literature written from the twelfth to the second century CE. When it was translated into Greek about 250 CE, other books known as the Apocrypha (a Greek word meaning 'hidden things') were included. This version, known as the Septuagint, was inherited by the Christian Church. During the Reformation in the sixteenth century (see unit 5) the Protestant churches rejected the Apocrypha, whilst the Roman Catholic Church kept it.

Another twenty-seven books were added by

Christians. These were written about Jesus and became known as the New Testament. So the Christian Bible is a library consisting of either sixty-six books or, if the thirteen books of the Apocrypha are added, seventy-nine books.

The Jewish scriptures

The Jewish scriptures, the Old Testament, are very important to both Jews and Christians. These scriptures were used by the Christians who included them in their own Bible. The New Testament writers often used the Old Testament writings to try to show that the history of Israel was a preparation for the coming of Jesus. From the Christian point of view the Jewish scriptures are of great importance, because they are seen as 'prophesying' (foretelling) the coming of Jesus.

The Gospels

The four Gospels each have the name of their traditional author – Matthew, Mark, Luke and John. The first three are similar in style, use material that is common to all three and are often called the 'synoptic Gospels'. There has been much debate about exactly when they were written, but most 'scholars' (experts) today agree that they were written between 60 and 110 CE, with Mark's Gospel being written first.

The Gospels tell of the work and life of Jesus, his teachings, his miracles, his death and resurrection. Each Gospel has its own special message. While there are differences in style and content, most Christians accept them all as contributing to a greater understanding of the meaning of Jesus' life.

Letters

As we saw in unit 4, *Letters* contains the Epistles written by St Paul – fourteen in all; and letters written by other early Christians. Generally *Letters* describes the main concerns of the early Christians and interprets the meaning of Jesus' life.

Revelation

This unique book is at the very end of the New Testament. It is written in a very poetic style and is full of powerful symbols. The book is written in the form of a kind of vision and describes the end of the world, the day of judgement (when God judges all the people of the earth) and the return of Jesus to earth.

Canon

The word **canon** is used to describe a collection of books which have the authority of a religious community. The Christian canon was not completed until 367 CE, mainly because there was much debate about whether the books of the New Testament were acceptable to the whole of the early Christian community.

The Bible in worship

The Bible is read every Sunday in every Christian place of worship throughout the world. Usually, the congregation (audience) hears two short readings during a service, one from the Old Testament and one from the New Testament. Many churches use a 'lectionary', a set of readings operating over the year. Each Sunday, different passages are selected for reading. This ensures that people who go to church listen to readings which otherwise they might never hear. During most services the **priest** or **minister** gives a 'sermon', a talk, quoting from the Bible and explaining the significance of the reading.

FOR YOUR FOLDERS

▶ Why do Christians believe that although the Gospels have differences, they all help people to understand more about the life of Jesus?
▶ Explain the following words: Bible; Apocrypha; synoptic; scholars; canon; lectionary.
▶ Why are the Jewish scriptures so important to Christians?
▶ Give some reasons why the Bible is important in Christian belief and practice.

7 THINKING ABOUT THE BIBLE

Although Christians might use other books, like hymn books and prayer books, in their faith and practices, the Bible has a special authority for them.

But what makes the Bible special? What makes it different from other books?

The Bible is the only book that Christians call 'the **word** of God'. This phrase may mean different things to different Christians. Within the Christian religion there are many different views about the Bible. In this section we shall be thinking about these different views.

Before doing this we need to ask another question. It concerns 'authority'. Where does final authority come from when deciding what is true Christian faith and practice? Generally, Christians believe that final authority comes from three sources:

- the Bible;
- the Church;
- individual conscience.

So, if and when Christians need some sort of answer or guideline to a particular question or problem, they will look to one, two, or perhaps all three of these sources. For example, many Roman Catholic Christians believe that the Church has the right to decide the correct interpretation of the Bible.

For them the authority of the Church may be stressed more than the authority of the Bible. Some Protestant Christians, on the other hand, might say that correct interpretation of the Bible depends on the Holy Spirit inspiring the reader. For them the authority of the Bible is stressed more than the authority of the Church.

Viewpoints on the Bible

- God guided the writers of the Bible to write down his will, word for word. The Bible is therefore without error.
- The Bible contains a record of the way God gradually made himself known more closely to people. Some of the ideas in the Bible might seem inconsistent. This is because God has gradually revealed his will to people, depending on their ability to understand it.
- God does not speak through any single word in the Bible, but rather through the great ideas and thoughts that are in the Bible. Some parts of the Bible are more valuable than others, but taken as a whole certain important ideas stand out above all others. For example, there is one God who created the universe; he is a God of love.

THINGS TO DO

▶ Read the two extracts below from the Sermon on the Mount. What ideas do you think they are trying to express? Do you think these ideas are relevant in our lives today?

About personal wrongs

'You have learned that they were told, "Eye for eye, tooth for tooth." But what I tell you is this: Do not set yourself against the man who wrongs you. If someone slaps you on the right cheek, turn and offer him your left. If a man wants to sue you for your shirt, let him have your coat as well. If a man in authority makes you go one mile, go with him two. Give when you are asked to give; and do not turn your back on a man who wants to borrow.'

(Matthew 5:38–42)

Judging others

'Pass no judgement, and you will not be judged. For as you judge others, so you will yourselves be judged, and whatever measure you deal out to others you will be dealt back to you. Why do you look at the speck of sawdust in your brother's eye, with never a thought for the great plank in your own? Or how can you say to your brother, "Let me take the speck out of your eye", when all the time there is that plank in your own? You hypocrite! First take the plank out of your own eye, and then you will see clearly to take the speck out of your brother's.

'Do not give dogs what is holy; do not throw your pearls to the pigs: they will only trample on them, and turn and tear you to pieces.'

(Matthew 7:1–5)

- The Bible contains great ancient knowledge about what it means to be human. It can all be read literally, but on a deeper level it speaks to each one of us about what we are and what we can possibly become.

The Bible and the modern world

How can a book that was written so long ago have any meaning for people now? Does it still have a message for the world today?

One reason for asking these questions is that many of the problems and issues facing us today are modern ones. The writers of the Bible knew nothing of nuclear weapons, surrogate motherhood, pollution, test-tubes babies, etc.

Very generally, Christians would answer these questions in the following ways:

- The message of the Bible is the same today as it always has been. Human nature does not change. The teachings in the Bible are **eternal**. They need to be applied to the world today.
- Those who wrote the Bible were addressing themselves to people and events thousands of years ago. We cannot simply accept what they said blindly, but rather we have to *interpret* the ideas in the Bible in the light of our understanding of the world today.

FOR YOUR FOLDERS

▶ Where do Christians believe that final authority comes from?

▶ How might Roman Catholic Christians and Protestant Christians differ in their views on authority?

▶ What problems might Christians who believe that every word in the Bible is correct face in respect of the *Genesis* account of creation? (see *Genesis* 1 – the first book in the Bible.)

▶ *'The teachings in the Bible are old-fashioned.'*

! *'Human nature does not change.'*
∙ In the light of these two statements do you think that the teachings in the Bible are relevant today?

'What I tell you is this: love your enemies and pray for your persecutors' (Matthew 5:43–44)

KEY QUESTIONS

Do you ever 'just feel' that there is 'something more to life'? Does the world ever seem so beautiful that you feel there is 'something more to life'? Are there times when you are so full of joy and happiness that you feel there is 'something more to life'? Are there times when you have felt such pain and unhappiness that this has taken you deep within yourself and you have began to feel that there is 'something more to life'? Or has this pain made you think that life is meaningless? Are there times when you hear a piece of music or see a painting or photograph that you feel deeply moved and can't explain in words what you feel? Are there times when you suddenly become aware of the miracle and beauty of nature and feel that there must be some sort of meaning and purpose in life?

For many people a belief in 'something more', or a power bigger than themselves, depends on their 'intuition', that is on their sensing something of this power. Throughout human history men and women have believed that as well as the world that we can see, the physical and external world, there is a spiritual and hidden internal world.

Sometimes people do not think that sensing this feeling is enough. They want firm proof. They want to have it proved to them that there is a power beyond everything else. But what is proof? Scientists, in setting about proving something, have ideas, and then set up experiments to show whether or not these ideas are correct. The scientists then give their conclusions – that is, whether or not the ideas were right. Is it possible to set up an experiment to prove the idea that there is a spiritual world, or that there is a power beyond everything else?

TALKING POINTS

- 'The last step of reason is to recognize that there are many things that lie beyond us.'
(Blaise Pascal)

Like all religions, Christianity teaches that there are many things that lie beyond our ordinary everyday sense experiences. Christianity teaches that there is within this world a spiritual dimension to life. It is against this background that we must look at the next few units on some of the basic Christian beliefs about God, the universe, the Holy Ghost, salvation, life after death and suffering. For, like all religious traditions, Christianity stresses that the world and the universe are the products of a supreme being, a creator, a God.

The Bible opens with the following words:

'In the beginning God created the heavens and the earth.'

(Genesis 1:1)

In other words, the universe came into being through the will of the divine. Everything in the universe is the manifestation (the revealed presence of a Spirit) of this divine will, this God.

For some centuries Christians and scientists have been engaged in much debate about questions like 'How did the universe come into being?' However, over the last few decades science and religion, rather than arguing about this and other questions, have begun to listen to each other and try to learn from each other. Often in the past they have been asking different questions: science asking 'How?' and religion asking 'Why?'. Two great twentieth-century scientists, Albert Einstein and Teilhard de Chardin both came to similar conclusions in their work, namely that the universe is not the product of pure blind chance, but rather of order, purpose and design.

Christians believe in a created world

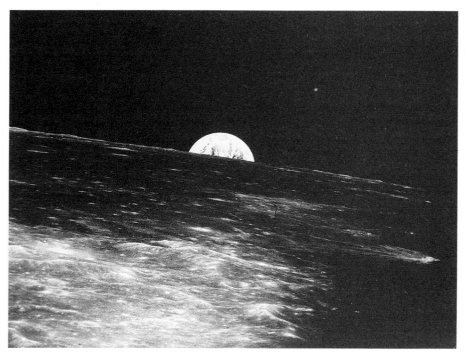

'When I see the glories of the cosmos I can't help but believe that there is a Divine Hand behind it all'   (Einstein)

'Nature is the art of God.'

(Teilhard de Chardin)

Poets and writers through the centuries have been concerned with ideas about God, the universe and the spiritual world. Here are a few reflections for you to look at and discuss:

FOR DISCUSSION

▶ After reading this unit discuss in groups of three or four some of the main ideas that have arisen.

REFLECTIONS

'It is hard to believe in God, but it is harder not to believe. I believe in God not from what I see in Nature but from what I find in man.'

(Tennyson)

'Amid the mysteries, there will remain the one absolute certainty, that we are ever in the presence of an Infinite and Eternal Energy from which all things proceed.'

(Spencer)

'No man can stand in the tropic forests without feeling that they are temples filled with the various productions of the God of nature, and that there is more in man than the breath of his body.'

(Charles Darwin)

'Millions of spiritual creatures walk the Earth Unseen, both when we wake and when we sleep.'

(John Milton)

'To see a World in a Grain of Sand And a Heaven in a Wild Flower, Hold Infinity in the palm of your hand And Eternity in an hour.'

(William Blake)

9 CENTRAL CHRISTIAN BELIEFS

I believe in God
the Father Almighty,
Maker of Heaven and earth,
And in Jesus Christ
His only Son our Lord,
who was conceived by the Holy Ghost,
Born of the Virgin Mary,
Suffered under Pontius Pilate,
Was crucified, dead and buried;
He descended into hell:
The third day he rose again from the dead;
He ascended into heaven,
And sitteth on the right hand of God the Father Almighty,
From thence he shall come to judge the quick and the dead.
I believe in
The Holy Ghost;
The Holy Catholic Church;
The Communion of Saints;
The forgiveness of sins;
The resurrection of the body;
And the life everlasting.

(Apostles' Creed)

If we look at the Apostles' Creed, which was formulated around 450 CE, we begin to see some of the central beliefs of the Christian religion.

In this unit we shall look at some of the main ideas concerning belief in God and the Holy Spirit. Unit 16 shows some central beliefs concerning Jesus Christ.

God

Christians believe in one God who revealed himself to the world as Father, Son and Holy Spirit. These are not three different gods, but rather different sorts of activity of God. The term **trinity** (see unit 3) is used to cover the activities of Father, Son and Holy Spirit.

Seven centuries ago an English writer whose name is still not known wrote a classic little book to which he or she gave the name *The Cloud of Unknowing*. In this book the writer said that however much people seem to know about God, this God must always remain unknown to us, or at least unknown to the thinking part of us (the 'intellect'). When it comes to the emotional part of us, and love, the writer said it is then a different matter:

> *'He may well be loved, but He may not be thought of.*
> *He may be reached and held close by means of love, but*
> *by means of thought, never.'*

(*The Cloud of Unknowing*)

'God must always remain in himself, unknown'

However, to Christians there are some ideas about God that help them to begin to understand him, and certain characteristics have been attributed (given) to God.

Traditionally these characteristics are that God is one; the creator; the uncaused cause; omnipotent (all powerful); omnipresent (present everywhere); omniscient (all knowing); eternal and unchanging; all loving; holy; perfect; willing to reveal his truths to his creation; a personal God.

The Holy Spirit

The Greek word which is translated 'spirit' can also mean 'wind' or 'breath'. In the Apostles' Creed the Holy Spirit is called the Holy Ghost; for Christians the Holy Spirit is an invisible force or power that makes them aware of powers beyond themselves. It is so powerful and so moving that it can change their lives and give them inner strength. Christian tradition has pointed to the Holy Spirit as:

- giving – inspiration, guidance, comfort, special gifts;
- revealing – God's truths, especially through the life of Jesus;
- being – creative, and a source of great holiness, power and love;
- active – through God's creation.

One particular church, the Pentecostal Church, places great emphasis on the day of Pentecost (see unit 4) when the first Christians experienced the power of the Holy Spirit (see Acts 2:2–4). In their worship the Pentecostalists try to rediscover the kinds of experiences which changed the lives of the first Christians. They believe that people can experience and become inspired by the power of the Holy Spirit and receive 'gifts of the spirit'. These can include the ability to heal people and to be able to speak in 'tongues', strange languages which cannot be understood. (Speaking in tongues is sometimes referred to as 'glossolalia'.)

FOR YOUR FOLDERS

▶ Look at some of the characteristics of God. In your own words try to explain what each of these words means.

! ▶ What do you think the author of *The Cloud of Unknowing* meant by the words *'but He may not be thought of'*?

▶ Explain in your own words what Christians believe about the Holy Spirit.

Christians believe in God, the creator

21

10 SUFFERING

You have probably already experienced both physical and mental suffering in your life. Suffering is part of life – no human being can escape it. Different people respond differently to others' suffering. Some typical responses might include: 'It's nothing to do with me'; 'I must try to help'; 'It's their own fault anyway'; 'It is through suffering that we learn to grow as human beings'. Many people are driven to ask the questions 'Why is there so much suffering in the world?' 'Why if there is a God does He allow such suffering?'.

The problem of evil

For theists (people who believe in God) the problem of suffering and evil poses some serious questions. Why does God allow evil? Why doesn't God do something about it? If God is all-powerful He must be able to prevent evil. If God is all-loving He must be willing to prevent evil. But if God is both able and willing to prevent evil, then why does evil exist?

Christian responses to the problem of evil

- The traditional Christian way of dealing with suffering is to say that after death all the suffering of this world will be forgotten in the joy of a new life.
- Suffering is caused by selfishness and self-centredness. This selfishness is called 'sin'. Sin is part of human nature and affects everyone. Sin does not mean simply doing something wrong, it is a whole attitude that leads people away from God.
- Human beings have free will: they are free to choose between good and evil. Suffering is caused by ignorance and blindness. If people became more aware of the world they live in and more aware of themselves and others, then the world could be free of such things as wars, disease, violence, famine, cruelty, injustice, torture, mental illness, brutality, pollution, racism, oppression, etc.

Belsen 1945. A victim of a concentration camp is thrown into a mass grave

- God suffers alongside people in the tragedies of the world.
- Suffering is part of life. It is only through suffering that people learn to grow as human beings. In a world without suffering there would be nothing to struggle for or against, nothing to strive for.
- Jesus Christ, the Son of God, was tortured to death. Yet Christians believe that He rose from the dead. Out of darkness and death came light and hope.
- Suffering is part of life. It is a challenge for us as individuals to find inner strength, and as part of the world community to try to make the world a better place.

Traditionally Christian thinkers have said that there are two types of suffering:

- moral – caused by human sin, ignorance and selfishness;
- natural – caused by natural phenomena like earthquakes, disease, floods, etc.

FOR YOUR FOLDERS

▶ Make a list of some examples of moral and natural suffering in the world today. Can you think of some suffering that could be avoided if people became more aware and less ignorant?

▶ Look at some of the Christian responses. What are your views on them?

▶ Write a description about the photograph. Why do events such as this make some people turn away from belief in a God?

TALKING POINTS

- 'From a distance the planet looks perfect. It is. Suffering is caused by human ignorance. We must learn to live in joy.'

- 'Imagine there's no heaven
it's easy if you try,
no hell below us
above us only sky.
Imagine all the people
living for today.
Imagine there's no country
it isn't hard to do
nothing to kill or die for
and no religion too.
Imagine all the people
living life in peace.
You may say I'm a dreamer
but I'm not the only one.
I hope some day you'll join us
and the world will be as one.
Imagine no possessions
I wonder if you can
no need for greed or hunger
a brotherhood of man.
Imagine all the people
sharing all the world.
You may say I'm a dreamer
but I'm not the only one.
I hope some day you'll join us
and the world will live as one.'

(**Imagine** by John Lennon)

A Christian funeral

Sometimes people don't like to think or talk about death, although it is an inevitable fact of life. Most people are afraid of death. One reason is that we have no idea of what's going to happen when we die. Fear of the unknown can be worse than fear of what we know.

KEY QUESTIONS

Is death the end? Is there a hell? Is there a heaven? Do we return to earth in another form? What is the soul?

Is death the end? From the dawn of human history people have answered 'No'. Long before there were any written records, there is evidence that people believed in some kind of life after death. Today all the world religions believe in life after death, although their beliefs can vary.

Very generally speaking, Christianity teaches that God is 'personal' – He has qualities like mercy, goodness and love. He cares for the people in His creation, who were created with the purpose of having a relationship with God. While this relationship can be entered into within this life, it can be fully realized only after this life. Salvation is thought of in terms of a personal relationship and fulfilment. Christians generally believe that they retain their personal identity and individuality after death. Judgement is an important idea. They believe that everyone will eventually have to account for what they've done in their lives. Traditionally, Christianity has taught that a good life will be rewarded in heaven and a bad life will be punished in hell. Roman Catholics believe that only those Christians who have led a very good life will

straightaway enter into heaven. Most will go to 'purgatory' – a type of purification process and preparation for heaven. Many modern Christians reject the idea of hell, and argue 'How could a God of love create a place of eternal suffering and torture?'. They believe that heaven is being with God. Hell is being apart from God. These are not places but rather states of mind.

For Christians, there is hope of eternal life confirmed by the life, death and resurrection of Jesus Christ. This 'eternal life' refers neither to infinite life, nor to immortality, but describes a quality of being. Life is eternal, because we are in continuing fellowship with God, through life before death and life after death.

Christian funerals

Some Christians are buried in coffins; others are cremated. It is traditional for people attending to wear dark clothes. Although there is sadness about death, the service stresses the hope that the dead person will in time be resurrected. Often the following words are read out at a funeral service:

'Lo! I tell you a mystery. We shall not all sleep, but we shall all be changed, in a moment, in the twinkling of an eye, at the last trumpet. For the trumpet will sound, and the dead will be raised imperishable, and we shall be changed. For this perishable nature must put on the imperishable, and this mortal nature must put on immortality. When the perishable puts on the imperishable, and the mortal puts on immortality, then shall come to pass the saying that is written:
"Death is swallowed up in victory."
"O death, where is thy victory?
O death, where is thy sting?"'

(1 Corinthians 15:51–55)

A dying Christian talks about death

David Watson was a vicar in the Church of England. On 5 January 1983 he discovered that he had cancer. He has since died, but before his death he wrote a book called *Fear No Evil*. Here are some of the things he said:

'With the fear of cancer so widespread in society, I was encouraged to write this book, giving an honest account of my feelings and reactions and how I have come to terms with cancer . . . I write unashamedly as a Christian, although I hope that my thoughts will be of some interest whatever faith a reader may have.'

WONDERFUL

'Certainly, for those who die in Christ the future will be unimaginably wonderful. The expression used several times is 'falling asleep' (see 1 Thessalonians 4:13–18). When we fall asleep after a tiring day, the next thing we know is waking refreshed the following morning. So it will be for the Christian. We fall asleep in Christ, and then wake up on the resurrection morning with our new spiritual bodies.'

LIKE TURNING ON A LIGHT

'If we think of all the best and most glorious moments in our lives the perfection of what we experience always seems just beyond our reach. As with striking a succession of matches to light a dark room, those moments invariably seem to flicker and fade. Heaven will be like turning on the full light. The perfection will be there for us to enjoy, undefiled, unflickering and unfading.'

THE CHRISTIAN IS PREPARING FOR LIFE

'In one sense, the Christian is not preparing for death. Essentially he is preparing for *life*, abundant life in all its fullness. The world, with its fleeting pleasures, is not the final reality, with heaven as a shadowy and suspect unknown. The best and purest joys on earth are only a shadow of the reality that God has prepared for us in Christ. Eternal life begins as soon as we receive Christ as our Saviour. We can start enjoying it now, in increasing measure, and should be preparing, not for death, but for the consummation of that perfect quality of life when we are completely in God's presence for ever.'

'In reality, when the body of the Christian dies, the really wonderful journey has only just begun.'

'Death for the Christian, it is sometimes said, is like the old family servant who opens the door to welcome the children home.'

'When I die, it is my firm conviction that I shall be more alive than ever . . .'

'The actual moment of dying is still shrouded in mystery, but as I keep my eyes on Jesus I am not afraid. Jesus has already been through death for us, and will be with us when we walk through it ourselves. In those great words of the Twenty-Third Psalm:

. . . Even though I walk through the valley of the shadow of death, I fear no evil; for thou art with me.'

(from Watson, D., *Fear No Evil*, Hodder and Stoughton)

12 SALVATION AND THE CHURCH

Salvation

PROFILE

'We are like prisoners trapped in a dark cell, locked away by our ignorance and selfishness, victims of our own negative emotions, like fear, anger, guilt. We are also faced with the enormous destructive powers outside of ourselves – violence, cruelty, disease, death. We feel powerless and so small in a huge world that often seems to be spinning out of control.

However, as a Christian, I believe that God is Love. There is no way that we, as individuals, can escape from this cell, but through God's **grace** we can be saved from darkness. Through the death and resurrection of Christ, God's son, we have all found salvation, and even death itself has been **redeemed**. The universe is not meaningless and God loves every human being on earth.'

(Jenny Taylor, student, author's interview)

KEY WORDS

Grace – the undeserving loving help that humanity receives from God.

Redeemed – ('Redemption' is from the Latin for 'brought back'.) Jesus is called 'Redeemer' because Christians believe that through his sacrifice on the cross people are now able to find their way back into full union with God.

Although Jenny Taylor's personal statement gives us an idea of Christian ideas about salvation, there are some differences of emphasis in what different Christians believe. The Orthodox and Roman Catholic emphasis is generally that the relationship between God and people only really begins to change when they become part of the Christian community. They can experience God's grace especially in the **sacraments** (see unit 21) and through the **Mass** (see unit 48). The Protestant emphasis is on *faith*. The new relationship between God and people does not depend on the rituals of the Church, but rather depends on the person having faith in Jesus Christ.

Christians believe that the universe has meaning

Although these differences might seem small they have been and still are the cause of controversy. Generally, however, most Christians would agree that:

- the relationship between God and people has been changed through the death and resurrection of Jesus;
- this relationship will be finally and completely changed in the future. Some Christians think of this future change as taking place after death. Others believe it will occur sometime in the future when Jesus will return to earth. (This is often called the 'second coming'.)

The Church

Among Christians there are three different ways of using the word '**Church**':
- the whole company of Christians since the time of Jesus;
- different groups or denominations;
- the local Christian community meeting regularly in a purpose-built building called a 'church'.

An image used to describe the Church is seen as being the physical body of Jesus Christ, continuing his work in the world.

In the Nicene Creed the Church is described as 'one, holy, catholic and apostolic':

- 'One' – Christians believe that unity in the Church is essential and it is the will of God that it should be one.
- 'Holy' – the Church is a sacred representation of God's will on earth. It provides the physical presence of Christ and continues His work in the world.
- 'Catholic' – this refers to the *universal* community of Christians.
- 'Apostolic' – the Church should be fulfilling the teachings of Jesus as handed down to the apostles of Jesus.

> *'Human suffering, the sum total of suffering poured out at each moment over the whole earth, is like an immeasurable ocean. But what makes up this immensity? Is it blackness; emptiness, barren wastes? No, indeed: it is potential energy. Suffering holds hidden within it, in extreme intensity, the ascensional force of the world. The whole point is to set this force free by making it conscious of what it signifies and of what it is capable. For if all the sick people in the world were simultaneously to turn their sufferings into a single shared longing for the speedy completion of the kingdom of God through the conquering and organizing of the earth, what a vast leap towards God the world would thereby make! If all those who suffer in the world were to unite their sufferings so that the pain of the world should become one single grand act of consciousness, of sublimation, of unification, would not this be one of the most exalted forms in which the mysterious work of creation could be manifested to our eyes?'*
>
> (Teilhard de Chardin,
> *Hymn of the Universe*, Collins, 1981)

FOR YOUR FOLDERS

▶ Explain the following words and phrases: grace; redemption; the second coming; body of Christ; catholic; apostolic.

▶ What different emphases on salvation are held by the churches?

▶ Briefly describe the different meanings of the word 'Church'.

13 'GO THEN, TO ALL PEOPLES EVERYWHERE'

Missionaries often became equated with white colonization

'Jesus drew near and said to them, . . . "Go then, to all peoples everywhere and make them my disciples"'
(Matthew 28:18, 19)

At the heart of the Christian belief is the idea that in Jesus, God has made the way of salvation possible for the people. Many Christians feel they have a duty to share this belief with all people, and there are Christian missionaries at work all over the world today. They believe they have a mission to help people discover Jesus Christ and accept him into their hearts. Christianity is often called a 'missionary religion'.

As with other beliefs and ideas, Christians have different views about mission and the task of the Church:

- The task of the Church is to convert people to the Christian life and make them members of the Church. Only through belief in Jesus Christ can people find salvation.
- The task of the Church is to 'plant' Christian communities in places where none existed

before. Local people should control their own churches.
- It is not up to the Church to convert people. God is already at work in the world where people are working for peace and justice.

'White souls'

During the seventeenth, eighteenth and nineteenth centuries Europe began to colonize the world. With its great wealth and power it began to carve up the world for its own economic and military gain. Alongside this colonial activity were the Christian missionaries who believed that there were millions of 'unfortunate pagans' who were desperately in need of conversion. As well as bringing their religion these missionaries brought with them European values and morals, often equating these values with godliness. Increasingly, missionaries became identified with white colonization and all the exploitation that this entailed. White

28

missionaries were often totally ignorant of the richness of the peoples' own cultures, histories and religions. Indeed, many of the attitudes of the missionaries seem to be far from 'Christian'.

'Did not Christ come into the world to make the souls if not the bodies of blacks inwardly white? Colonial expansion was a kind of final crusade against the children of darkness . . . whiteness itself was assumed to be the norm, dark skins deviations from the norm.'
(Alan Davies 'The Ideology of Racism', in Baum, G. and Coleman, J. *The Church and Racism*, Concilium 151, T and T Clark 1982)

The hope of spreading Christianity was linked with changing attitudes to race. After Darwin's *The Origin of Species* was published in 1859 it appeared possible to fit the non-European races into Darwin's theory of the survival of the fittest. If human history, like natural history, was governed by the survival of the fittest, the races of the West, with their advanced technology, had appeared to survive more effectively. Clearly therefore their Christian duty was to extend their leadership throughout the world. There can be little doubt that much missionary work, through ignorance and arrogance about racial and cultural superiority, caused a great deal of suffering

To their credit many missionaries worked to combat slavery and helped to bring the benefits of western know-how like medical services and education. By the 1920s many missionaries, particularly in Africa, were beginning to see that their most important task was to help the peoples of Africa prepare for self-government.

A multi-faith society

Over the last few decades in Britain there has been a growth in the number of people who follow religions other than Christianity. The growth of our multi-faith society has made many Christians reconsider their beliefs about missionary activities. Very generally two different approaches to this matter can be found among Christians:

- All religions are different paths to salvation. One religion is not 'superior' in any way to another. Therefore the Church's mission is not to try and convert the followers of these other religions. Its mission is to understand others, learn from them and share ideas about the meaning of life.

- Ultimately the only way to God and salvation is through belief in Jesus Christ. Followers of other religions are not wrong but can only go a short way on the path to fully understanding God.

FOR DISCUSSION

▶ 'Within a few years of white Christian settlers and their missionaries stepping foot in Australia, 600 000 Aborigines died. The destruction of aboriginal culture with its spiritual roots of wisdom planted deep within its sacred land, was on an appalling scale.' (John Pilger)

TALKING POINT

- **'There will be no peace among the peoples of this world without peace among the world religions.'**

(Hans Küng)

FOR YOUR FOLDERS

▶ Why do many Christians believe that their religion is a 'missionary' one?
▶ Briefly explain the different views about mission and the task of the Church.
▶ *'Christian missionary activity has in the past been equated with economic exploitation, cultural rape and racism.'* Explain what you think this statement means.
▶ What is a 'multi-faith' society? How has it affected the way many Christians see the role of the Churches?

14 DIALOGUE IN OUR GLOBAL VILLAGE

Christianity is just one of the world's major religions. In the world today there are millions of people who follow Hinduism, Islam, Buddhism, Judaism, Sikhism and other religions. Some of these religions are older than Christianity, whereas others like Islam and Sikhism have developed since Christianity.

Because we live in a global village dialogue is important

In the past there has often been conflict and strife between these religions and they have sometimes been the cause of wars and violence. Missionaries from some religions have tried to convert people of other religions and everyone else to their beliefs. Some people who follow their own religion have shown little regard or sympathy for other religions, believing that is it their religion which is the 'true' one and all the others are false. This attitude has often been the result of ignorance and a refusal to look at the beliefs and ideas of other religions.

Christians have often been guilty of this, regarding followers of other religions as being 'heathens' or 'infidels' or 'pagans'. This has been a dangerous attitude because it has often bred intolerance and misunderstanding. Indeed there are still today some Christians who strongly believe that the *only* way to God and salvation is through belief in Jesus Christ and that all other ways are of little worth. This attitude, which disregards other people's faith, is deeply destructive and divisive.

Human beings have often been called 'religious animals'. This means that through every period of

history, and in every culture in every part of the world, people have believed in forces and powers that lie beyond and within this world. We have as a species been powerfully aware of a 'spiritual world'. The way that this belief in a spiritual world has been expressed in ideas and practices has varied with different cultures. In Tibet, India, Palestine, China, Africa and Australia, in fact in places all over the world, these beliefs in a spiritual dimension to life have been expressed through the cultural influences of the country. The external practices might seem very different but many scholars believe that beneath the externals there is an underlying similarity of belief.

In the past, although these religious beliefs have met through trade, 'voyages of discovery' and sometimes missionary work, people often still clung on to the idea that their religion was the 'true' one and little was done to explore and exchange ideas.

However, today we live in a 'global village'. The world has got smaller, not geographically but in the sense that communication and travel have developed. We are far more knowledgeable about other parts of the world and their peoples. We can travel across the world in a matter of hours. We can switch on the television and see pictures from China. With this increased knowledge has come an awareness that people in different parts of the world have their own beliefs, ideas, cultures and customs. These are as important to them as ours are to us. The second part of the twentieth century has witnessed, among religions, a growing awareness of other religions and a growing desire to have 'dialogue': to talk, listen and learn about and from other religions. Also, because many people from places like India and Pakistan have settled in Britain, there has been a growing awareness of their beliefs and customs.

Although each religion is unique and has its own patterns of belief and practices, there is a growing awareness that there are similarities between them too.

Look at these sayings from the sacred scriptures of Hinduism, Judaism, Islam and Christianity:

'The life, or self, of this whole universe, is the same as that tiny seed from which it came. You are that self.'
(Upanishad 6:12:3)

'The Lord is near to all who call upon him, to all who call upon him in truth.'
(Psalm 145:18)

'We (God) are nearer to him (man) than his jugular vein.'
(Sura 50:15)

'The Kingdom of God is within you.'

(Luke 17:21)

Dialogue between the world religions is slowly beginning to increase. One of Christianity's leading theologians, Hans Küng, writes:

'If we compare interreligious dialogue (dialogue between the world religions) *with interconfessional dialogue* (dialogue between the various Christian churches) *we have to admit that we are now roughly at the same stage in interreligious dialogue that we were about fifty years ago in interconfessional dialogue. It is a slow process, but we are overcoming our isolation and learning to grasp the reality of others.'*

(Küng, H., *Christianity and the World Religions,*
William Collins Sons & Co 1987)

In the past, Christianity has tended to adopt a standpoint of 'exclusivity' which has been a blanket condemnation of other faiths and their truths, or a standpoint of 'superiority' which rates Christianity as 'better'. Küng and other Christian scholars believe that in this dialogue all the religions must realize that they have a lot to learn from others, and can teach others as well. This is not to say that they want to make all religions the same or aim to make one world religion, but simply to learn what others have to say. By doing this they can deepen their understanding of their own faith.

However, there will undoubtedly always be problems. For instance, many Christians interpret the following words in John's Gospel as meaning that ultimately the only way to God is through following Jesus Christ:

'I am the way; I am the truth and I am life; no one comes to the Father except by me.'

(John 14:6)

Some Christians, however, might interpret this differently, saying that there is a deeper inner meaning which has nothing to do with making Christianity exclusive in any way.

TALKING POINTS

- 'I have spread my dreams under your feet; Tread softly because you tread on my dreams.'

   (W.B. Yeats)

- 'All truth and light comes from the word of God, by Jesus, Isaiah, Buddha, Confucius, Mohammed. There is only one Divine Light – and every man in his own measure is enlightened by it.'

   (Archbishop William Temple)

- 'Wherever the teachings of all the religions of the world strike the eternal core of humanity, the teachings of Jesus, Mohammed, Lao-Tzu, The Buddha, are all the same. There is only one religion. There is only one happiness. There are a thousand forms, a thousand heralds, but only one call, one voice. The voice of God does not come just from the Bible. The essence of love, beauty and holiness does not reside in Christianity or in antiquity – it resides in you and me, in each one of us. This is the one eternal truth. It is the doctrine of the "Kingdom of Heaven" that we bear within ourselves. Demand more of yourselves. Love and joy and the mysterious things we call happiness are not over here or over there, they are only "within ourselves".'

   (Herman Hesse, *If the War Goes on,* Picador**)**

FOR YOUR FOLDERS

- ▶ After reading this unit write an article called 'Inter-faith dialogue in our global village'.
- ▶ Why do you think many people see such dialogue as being so important?

15 THE VIRGIN MARY

For millions of Christians, the Virgin Mary, is a beloved figure. Shrines to the Virgin Mary exist in many parts of the world, especially in Ireland, around the Mediterranean and in South America. Thousands of churches around the world have been named after her. Many Christians, down the ages, have reported seeing visions of Mary, e.g. at Lourdes (see unit 52). If we look at the Roman Catholic **Catechism** we can begin to understand her importance:

Who is the greatest of the saints?
The greatest of the saints is Mary, the virgin mother of God, also called Our Lady, who, by accepting the mother-hood of Jesus, brought God's salvation to the world. When being told by the angel that she was to be mother of the Saviour, she said: 'Behold, the handmaid of the Lord; be it done unto me according to thy word' (Lk 1:38).

What is the commonest prayer to Our Lady?
The commonest prayer to Our Lady is the 'Hail Mary': Hail Mary, full of grace, the Lord is with thee; blessed art thou amongst women and blessed is the fruit of thy womb, Jesus. Holy Mary, mother of God, pray for us sinners now and at the hour of our death. Amen.

What is the doctrine of the Assumption?
The doctrine of the Assumption is that in Mary our liberation from death, our resurrection, is anticipated; for her redemption is such that, like her Son, she is already humanly alive in heaven.

Why do we especially pray to Mary?
We especially pray to Mary, the mother of God, because Jesus on the cross gave her to us as our mother, for she is the type or image of our mother the Church and shows us, in her life, what God does for those he loves and redeems.

(*Roman Catholic Catechism*, Catholic Truth Society, 1985)

Mary is given a unique place in both the Roman Catholic Church and the Orthodox Churches. She is regarded as being a link between heaven and earth and because she is the mother of Jesus, she has special access to him. Roman Catholic and Orthodox Christians believe that she can and does 'intercede' (speak in favour) with Jesus, on behalf of people who pray to her.

Mary was given the title 'Mother of God' ('Theotokos' in Greek) in 431 CE as a sign of her special role. Roman Catholic and some Orthodox Christians believe that Jesus' birth caused her no pain. They believe that since the Holy Spirit, rather than a man gave her the seed of creation, she was a virgin, and she remained a virgin all her life.

These churches also believe that Mary's body was taken up to heaven when she died. This is called the **Assumption**. A feast day is held on 15 August to celebrate Mary's Assumption.

An artist's impression of Mary interceding on behalf of humanity

The Immaculate Conception

The Roman Catholic Church teaches that Mary, alone of all human beings since Adam and Eve, was born without sin, and remained free from sin all her life. They believe that no ordinary sinful person could have given birth to God's only Son, and so Mary must have been free from sin. This is called the **Immaculate Conception**.

Orthodox Christians do not hold this view. They believe that Mary was human, not sinless.

Mary in the Gospels

There is not a great deal about Mary in the Gospels. The Gospel's of Matthew and Luke record the birth of Jesus and they stress that Mary was an important person. She is mentioned a few times in the Gospel stories about Jesus' teaching and crucifixion.

Roman Catholic Christians stress that they do not actually worship Mary but honour her highly because of her place in God's plan for the world. Many Protestant Christians, however, feel uncomfortable about Mary's role, and this has led to great controversy in the past. However, today some Protestant Churches are willing to discuss her role and an Ecumenical Society of the Virgin Mary now exists.

These conflicting beliefs about the Virgin Mary highlight the way that Roman Catholic and Protestant Christians view authority. Since ideas like the Assumption and the Immaculate Conception are not actually written down in the Bible, Protestant Christians do not give them any authority. However, for Roman Catholics a major source of authority is the Church and its traditions. They believe that because these ideas are part of the Church's tradition, they do have great authority.

FOR YOUR FOLDERS

▶ Write about the importance of the Virgin Mary for Roman Catholic and Orthodox Christians.
▶ What are the similarities and differences of beliefs about the Virgin Mary among Christians?
! ▶ Why do some of these differences exist?

FOR DISCUSSION

▶ To many writers and artists throughout the ages, the Virgin Mary has been a figure who has been accorded great respect. In this extract Nikos Kazantzakis expresses this respect for her.

'Mary sat on a high stool in the tiny yard of her house. She was spinning. It was still bright outside: the summer light drew slowly away from the face of the earth and did not wish to leave. Mary spun and her mind twirled now this way, now that – together with the spindle. Memory and imagination joined: her life seemed half truth, half fable. The petty round of daily tasks had lasted for years and then suddenly the stunning uninvited peacock – the miracle – had come and covered her tormented existence with its long golden wings.

A brilliantly white dove flew down from the roof opposite, beat its wings for a moment over her head and then alighted with dignity on the pebbles of the yard and began to walk methodically round Mary's feet. It spread its tail-feathers, bent its neck, turned its head and looked at Mary, its round eye flashing in the evening light like a ruby. It looked at her – spoke to her. She called the bird in a very tender voice, and the delighted dove took a hop and landed on her joined knees.

Mary placed her hand on the dove which sat upon her knees. Caressing the dove, she struggled to bring the lightning back to mind after thirty years and to untangle its hidden meaning. She closed her eyes. In her palm she felt the dove's tiny warm body and beating heart . . . Suddenly – she did not realize how, she did not know why – dove and lightning were one; she was sure of it: the heartbeats and the thunder – all were God. Now for the first time she was able to make out the words hidden in the thunder, hidden in the dove's cooing: "Hail Mary . . . Hail Mary." Without a doubt, this was what God had cried: "Hail Mary."

(Nikos Kazantzakis, *Last Temptation*, Faber & Faber, 1975)

16 JESUS – HIS MESSAGE

We live in what is often called the 'technological age'. Modern science and technology have enabled human beings to do the most remarkable things, such as space exploration, the transplantation of human organs, satellite links and global communication, the invention of microchips and complex computer systems, world travel in a matter of hours, the splitting of the atom and the creation of nuclear weapons. As far as scientific and technological knowledge goes, human evolution has certainly been remarkable.

We live in a world that is full of conflict and human misery. Two-thirds of the world's people go hungry; wars and violence rage all over the world; pollution threatens to make the planet earth uninhabitable; our psychiatric hospitals are full of sad and confused individuals; people are cruel to each other in thoughts, words and deeds. As far as knowledge about ourselves and the way we treat others goes, human beings have a lot to learn.

We live in a world in which, especially in the technologically advanced west, we like to think that we've found the answers to the great mysteries of life. Yet we only have to pick up a newspaper or watch the news on television, or experience conflict and pain in our own lives, our homes and communities to realize that we indeed have a lot to learn.

Yet, because we are human, we still search for the answers to questions that have always puzzled humanity. How can we develop as individuals? How can we learn to get on with others? How can we find peace of mind within ourselves? How should we try to live in this huge, confusing world of ours?

An important part of all sacred writings from all religious traditions is concerned with these sorts of questions. Christians look to the teachings of Jesus Christ as laid out in the Gospels to give them guidance as to how they should live. Christians, and many non-Christians too, believe that the finest example of an ideal person was the life and teachings of Jesus. All the qualities that make up the ideal person are to be found in the way he lived, his attitude towards others and his devotion to God.

The teachings in the Bible are basically about humanity rising above the violence that characterizes our present existence

Jesus' teachings are challenging. They require self-sacrifice and service. In fact they are so challenging and so demanding that few people in the world today or in the past have been able to follow them completely. In the Gospels the teachings set an *ideal* – something people should try to aim for. If we look at the following teachings, for example, we find that this ideal requires that people have to change the way they think and act:

'Love your enemies.'

(Matthew 5:44)

'Love your neighbour as yourself.'

(Mark 12:31)

'A man can have no greater love than to lay down his life for his friends.'

(John 15:13)

'If anyone hit's you on the right cheek offer him the other as well.'

(Matthew 5:39)

'Go and sell everything you own and give the money to the poor, and you will have treasure in heaven.'

(Mark 10:21)

'Do not judge and you will not be judged, because the judgements you give are the judgements you will get.'

(Matthew 7:1)

'It is easier for a camel to pass through the eye of a needle than for a rich man to enter the Kingdom of God.'

(Mark 10:25, 26)

'When they reached the place called The Skull, they crucified him there and the two criminals also, one on the right, the other on the left. Jesus said, "Father forgive them; they do not know what they are doing."'

(Luke 23:33, 34)

There can be little doubt that few people live out these teachings in their daily lives. In the Gospels Jesus teaches that people need to change from within themselves. This idea is often referred to in the Gospels as 'being reborn'. The teachings in the Gospels are basically about humanity rising above the violence which characterizes our present existence and working towards developing and

evolving as human beings. They teach that humanity is capable of undergoing a definite inner development and evolution. This inner evolution requires that people become more understanding and aware of themselves, of others, of the world and of God.

If people work towards the ideal that Jesus sets in the Gospels, then the world, with all its conflict and violence can begin to change for the better.

FOR DISCUSSION

► 'Always treat others as you would like them to treat you.'

(Jesus)

FOR YOUR FOLDERS

► *'As far as knowledge about ourselves and the way we treat others goes, human beings have a lot to learn.'* What do you think this statement means? Can you think of examples from the world today that back up this statement?
► Why do you think Jesus' teachings are often said to be challenging?
► Read the eight quotes from the Gospels again. In a world of violence, revenge, anger, selfishness, pride, poverty and injustice, what might happen to this world if people really began to be 'reborn' and were able to apply these teachings to their daily lives?

TALKING POINT

● 'The longest journey
Is the journey inwards.'

(Dag Hammarskjöld)

REFLECTIONS

'The Roman Catholic church has given continuous guidance and interpretation of God's word down the centuries; Protestants are more likely to refer straight back to biblical fundamentals. Both methods possess their virtues, but if they are to be true to the springs of Christianity, the absolute principal from which they seek guidance can only be love.'

(John St John, Religion and Social Justice, Pergamon Press 1985)

'If Christianity had to be defined in one word, then this word would be "love".'

(Mother Teresa)

'There are three words for "love" in the Greek New Testament; one is the word "eros". Eros is a sort of romantic love. There is and can always be something beautiful about eros. Some of the most beautiful love in all the world has been expressed this way.

Then the Greek language talks about "philos", which is another word for love – a kind of intimate love between friends. This is the kind of love you have for those people that you get along with well, and those whom you like on this level you love because you are loved.

Then the Greek language has another word for love, and that is the word "agape". Agape is more than romantic love, it is more than friendship. Agape is understanding, creative, redemptive goodwill towards all people. Agape is an overflowing love that seeks nothing in return. Theologians would say that it is the love of God operating in the human heart. When you rise to love on this level, you love all men not because you like them, not because their ways appeal to you, but you love them because God loves them. This is what Jesus meant when he said, "Love your enemies". And I'm happy that he didn't say, "Like your enemies", because there are some people that I find it very difficult to like. Liking is an affectionate emotion, and I can't like anyone who would bomb my home. I can't like anyone who would exploit me. I can't like anyone who would trample over me with injustices. I can't like them. But Jesus reminds us that love is greater than liking. Love is understanding, creative, redemptive goodwill towards all people.'

(Dr Martin Luther King 'A Christmas Sermon', from the Trumpet of Conscience, Hodder and Stoughton 1967)

'Love is patient; love is kind and envies no one. Love is never boastful nor conceited, nor rude; never selfish, not quick to take offence. Love keeps no score of wrongs; does not gloat over other men's sins, but delights in the truth. There is nothing love cannot face; there is no limit to its faith, its hope, and its endurance. Love will never come to an end.'

(St Paul, 1 Corinthians 13:4–8)

'Love can adapt itself to every phase of a changing world.'

(Paul Tillich)

'This was it, the sense and meaning of the universe; it was love . . . It was for me to justify the world by loving and forgiving it; to discover its meaning through love.'

(P. Dumitriu)

'God loved the world so much that he gave his only Son, . . .'

(John 3:16)

'I give you a new commandment: love one another; as I have loved you, so you are to love one another.'

(John 13:34)

'Only by revolution, by changing the concrete conditions of our country, can we enable men to practise love for each other.'

(Father Camilo Torres)

'In order to be able to love and to change the world for the better, we need to get in touch with agape, and to be aware that human life, nature, our planet, the entire cosmos is essentially one and that behind it and sustaining it is another reality beyond our understanding . . . life on earth is threatened. Love, if it is true to itself, must always be effective. It is the expression of love, the putting into practice what love demands which is all important.'

(John St John, Religion and Social Justice, Pergamon Press 1985)

FOR YOUR FOLDERS

In this unit are reflections on the meaning of Christian love. After reading these reflections answer the following questions:

▶ Explain 'eros', 'philos' and 'agape'.
▶ Which different types of love do they refer to?
▶ What is Christianity all about according to Mother Teresa?
▶ What are the qualities that St Paul attributes to love?
▶ In St John's Gospel what is Jesus' new commandment?

▶ For many Christians love (agape) compels them to become involved in the problems facing all people. Try to explain in your own words the statements of Camilo Torres and John St John. What do you think are the major problems facing the world?
▶ Write down some thoughts about love. Discuss them with a friend.

'If Christianity had to be defined in one word, then this word would be love' (Mother Teresa)

18 SERVICE AND SACRIFICE

'Greater love has no man than this, that a man lay down his life for his friends.'

(John 15:13)

Throughout history people have sometimes felt so strongly about something that they are prepared to dedicate their whole lives to their beliefs, and sometimes even willing to die for their beliefs.

Sometimes these beliefs may mean that they do things that are not morally acceptable to others. However, when people act on beliefs that do no harm to others and are part of an attempt to make the world a more peaceful, just and fair place then these people deserve our respect.

People who are willing to die for their beliefs are usually called **martyrs**. They believe that some force or ideal far greater than their own lives calls them to make a sacrifice of themselves.

The Christian Church has always recognized that certain people are especially holy, because they have lived a life that is very close to the Christian ideal. The Church has traditionally called these people 'saints'. A saint is someone who has lived a holy or completely unselfish life and is officially recognized after death as being worthy of special honour. The Roman Catholic and Orthodox Churches officially recognize that a person has lived the life of a saint by a process called 'canonization'. The Church authorities study every aspect of the dead person's life in great detail before deciding whether to make that person a saint. However, not everyone who has lived such a good life is known to the authorities, and so on 1 November all these people are honoured in the Feast of All Saints.

In this unit we shall look at profiles of four twentieth-century Christians whose faith has inspired them to live lives of self-sacrifice and service to others.

Martin Luther King

Maximilian Kolbe

Mother Teresa

Oscar Romero

Oscar Romero

Oscar Romero was Archbishop in El Salvador where the government has consistently violated human rights. Most of the people live in desperate poverty, and in order to keep power the government has brutally and cruelly crushed any opposition. Despite many threats against his life, Romero spoke out against the government in sermons. In 1980 he was gunned down by four masked men while he celebrated mass in his cathedral. His last words were, *'May Christ's sacrifice give us the courage to offer our own bodies for justice and peace'*.

Mother Teresa of Calcutta

For over forty years, this nun has totally dedicated her life to helping the destitute and dying people of Calcutta. Her Christian faith has inspired her to live in the slums and share her life with the poor. She says, *'What these people need even more than food and shelter is to be wanted. They understand that even if they only have a few hours left to live, they are loved. Make us worthy Lord, to serve those throughout the world who live and die poor and hungry'*.

Maximilian Kolbe

Maximilian Kolbe was a Polish Catholic priest who was arrested and taken to Auschwitz, one of the Nazi death camps, in 1941. Auschwitz was a living hell – thousands of people died every day from beatings, torture, disease, starvation or in the gas chambers. Priests were especially ill-treated and on one occasion Father Kolbe was stripped naked and whipped fifty times. One day the guards picked out a man to be tortured to death. Father Kolbe stood and said, 'Take me instead'. He was stripped and thrown into a stinking hole and starved to death. His heroism echoed through the camp. In 1982 he was made a saint. He once said, *'My aim in life is to serve others'*.

Martin Luther King

Dr Martin Luther King was an American Baptist minister. He was dedicated to trying to change the way that black people were treated in America. They earned half as much as white people; many were not allowed to vote; they were not allowed into certain public places that were reserved for whites only. Despite many death threats he organized campaigns, boycotts, marches and other forms of peaceful protest to bring justice for the black people of America. In 1965 equal voting rights were given to the black people. In 1968, when he was only 39, he was assassinated. His life and his vision of a peaceful and fairer world have become an inspiration for oppressed people all over the world. In a speech he once said, *'I have a dream that one day all God's children, blacks, whites, Jews, Gentiles, Protestants and Catholics, will be able to join hands and sing in the words of the black people's old song, Free at last, free at last, thank God Almighty, we are free at last'*.

The hidden multitude

Of course there have been tens of thousands of courageous men and women who have not become known, whose faith has inspired their lives and the lives of others. This prayer, by a poet unknown, was found scribbled on a piece of wrapping paper near the body of a dead child at Ravensbruk concentration camp, one of the Nazi death camps of the second world war.

A Prisoner's Prayer
O, Lord,
remember not only the men and women of good will
but also those of evil will.
But do not remember all the suffering
they have inflicted upon us;
remember the fruits we have borne
thanks to this suffering –
our comradeship, our loyalty, our humility,
our courage, our generosity,
the greatness of heart
which has grown out of all this;
and when they come to the judgement,
let all the fruits that we have borne
be their forgiveness.

FOR YOUR FOLDERS

► Oscar Romero spoke of 'Christ's sacrifice'. What was Christ's sacrifice?

! How do you think Christ's sacrifice has inspired Christians to struggle against injustice and oppression?

► Write an essay, using these profiles, called 'Service and sacrifice in the twentieth century'.

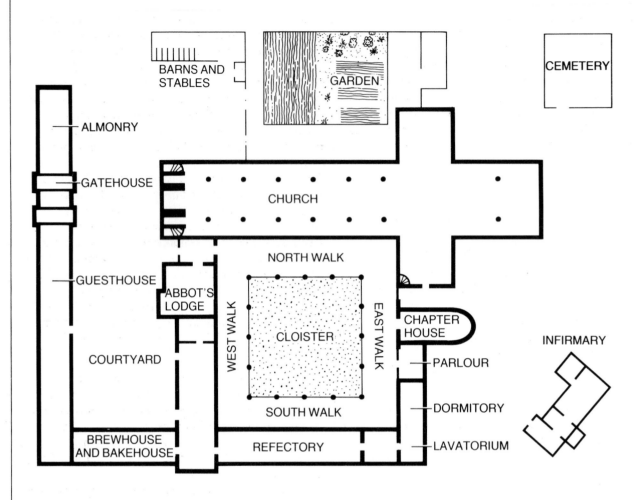

Plan of a typical Benedictine monastery

A typical day in a Benedictine monastery

LAUDS : PRAISE MORNING PRAYER

PRIME : FIRST HOUR 6 AM

TERCE : THIRD HOUR 9 AM

SEXT : SIXTH HOUR NOON

NONE : NINTH HOUR 3 PM

VESPERS : EVENING EVENING PRAYER

COMPLINE : COMPLETE FINAL NIGHT PRAYER

Long before the rise of Christianity, 'monasticism' existed in many parts of the world. Monasticism means that people live in seclusion, obeying religious vows they have taken. The first Christian hermits lived alone in the deserts. By about 530 CBE an Italian called Benedict had founded a monastery. He wrote a set of rules for the monastic life and these rules became known as the Rule of St Benedict. They covered every aspect of monastic life and St Benedict described the monastery as 'a school of the service of the Lord'.

Over the centuries other monastic orders were formed. In 1209 St Francis formed the Franscican Order. He set out to form an order of brothers who would be carefree disciples of Jesus living in poverty. During the same period, Dominic, a Spanish priest, founded the Dominican Order. His brothers too were travelling preachers, seeking learning and knowledge, but they did not endure the same level of poverty as Francis' brothers.

Members of religious communities take vows of poverty, chastity, obedience and prayer. The monastic day is filled with prayer, reading, meditation, worship and many different types of work involving much manual labour. Over the centuries Christian women have become involved in their own religious communities called convents – places where nuns live according to their religious vows.

People who join religious communities have made a personal commitment to dedicate their whole lives, minds, bodies and souls to worshipping God and developing themselves as spiritual men and women. A monastic life is not an escape from the world. People living in such close proximity to each other have to face all the problems that human relationships cause; they have to work hard and monks and nuns do a whole range of different types of work.

One of the most famous Christian monks of this century was the Trappist monk called Thomas Merton. The Trappist order have taken a vow of silence, along with their other vows. Merton's writings have had a great influence on the lives of many Christians. Ironically Merton, a member of a silent order, played an important part in the political and social protests of his times, including the struggle for racial equality in the USA, and in the struggle against nuclear weapons and the Vietnam War. He explained this involvement in one of his books:

> 'This is an age that, by its very nature at a time of crisis, of revolution, of struggle, which calls for the special searching and questioning which are the work of the monk in his meditation and prayer . . . the monk abandons the world only in order to listen more intently to the deepest and most neglected voices that proceed from its inner depths.'
>
> (Thomas Merton, *Contemplative Prayer*, Darton, Longman and Todd 1975)

REFLECTIONS

'When I was sixteen I realized that I had to be a nun. There was no sudden flash; it was rather as if the truth had been there in my mind for a long time. I believe we are chosen, but that also experience of God can come through events that are part of the weave of our ordinary lives.'

(Dame Maria Boulding)

'When people ask me why I became a monk, I feel very like the engaged couple who are asked why they have fallen in love. We don't really know. Certain things happen in our lives which make us come to a decision.'

(Dom Leonard Vickers)

SAMPLES OF BENEDICT'S RULES

'Above all, let not the evil of grumbling appear, on any account, by the least sign or word whatever.'
'Let the monks sleep clothed girdled with belts or cords – but without knives at their sides lest they injure themselves in sleep. And thus let the monks be always ready; when the signal is given, let them rise without delay.'

FOR YOUR FOLDERS

▶ Briefly explain who Benedict, Francis and Dominic were.
▶ Look at the plan of a Benedictine monastery. Using a dictionary write a sentence to say what takes place in the cloister, the infirmary, the rectory and the chapter house.
▶ *'People who join religious communities are not escaping from the world but rather confronting it.'* Comment on this statement.

20 THE CONTEMPLATIVE LIFE

Brother David

As we have seen in the last unit, people who join religious communities are engaged in many different types of activity. One very important feature of life for monks and nuns is **contemplation**. This can take many forms, but generally it entails thinking deeply and quietly about the meaning of life. The word '**contemplative**' applies to the individual's spiritual life. Thomas Merton describes the contemplative life in this reflection.

REFLECTION

'When I talk about the contemplative life I am talking about a special dimension of inner discipline and experience, a fullness of personal development which are not compatible with a purely external busy-busy existence. This is not incompatible with action, with creative work, with dedicated love. These all go together. Real Christian living is stunted if it remains content with the bare externals of worship, with "saying prayers" and "going to church" and merely being respectable. The real purpose of contemplation is to deepen one's love, one's awareness of God, of exploration, discovery and illumination. What is the relation of this to action? Simply this. He who attempts to act and do things for others or for the world without deepening his own self-understanding and capacity to love, will not have anything to give others.'

(*Thomas Merton, Contemplation in a World of Action, George Allen and Unwin Australia, 1980*)

KEY WORDS

Contemplation – 'to think deeply; to consider with attention; to look at quietly; deep thought.'
Contemplative – 'someone who spends much time in contemplation.'
(*Longman's Dictionary of Contemporary English*)

FOR YOUR FOLDERS

▶ After reading the extracts in this unit explain what the contemplative life means for Thomas Merton and Brother David.
▶ What does Brother David mean by:
   a uprootedness;
   b spiritual;
   c flesh?
▶ Do you agree with some of the things he says?
▶ Do you think that most of 'our time' we are not 'rooted in time at all'? What do you think it means not to be rooted in time?

In this reflection, Brother David, a member of the Benedictine Order, explains his beliefs about the spiritual life.

REFLECTION

If we speak about the spiritual work of our time, there are three questions I would like to ask. What characterizes our time? What is the spiritual work for our time? And, how are we to go about it?

If we ask what characterizes our time, I offer one word: uprootedness.

Think, for instance, of the uprootedness that comes as a by-product of mobility. Now, it is very good that we can move quickly and easily from place to place. But there are families in the United States who move more than 20 times while their children are growing up. Think of our uprootedness from our families. There are many people who have had little or no contact with their grandparents, who hardly know their names.

Or think of our uprootedness from the Earth. Do you know the garden from which your fruits and vegetables come? How many people in the world know the well from which their water comes? They never give a thought to it, yet this used to be rather important.

Think of our uprootedness from our bodies and what it takes to experience our bodies as the embodiment of spirit and of our lives and to experience ourselves as body-spirits.

How many of us can say with conviction that we are really rooted in a tradition, rooted in the sense of getting nourishment from it?

We are speaking of our time. How rooted are we in time at all? Most of the time, 48% of us is clinging to the past, 51% is stretching out frantically towards the future and 1% is left to be present where we are in this moment. So, it isn't even our time; it's just passing us by while we are busy with nostalgic memories or impatient fantasies.

How can we root ourselves in time? By facing first of all, the problem of our uprootedness; facing the challenge that emerges from it; and therefore facing the task. The task is re-rooting ourselves — in a place, in social structures, in this Earth, in our body, in tradition, in time.

When people say 'spiritual' they mean a great variety of things, so we ought to ask ourselves what we mean by spiritual. It means aliveness. Spiritual means alive – super-alive, if you want.

The opposite of spirit is not matter. Absolutely not. St Paul speaks of a 'spiritual rock'. If a rock can be spiritual, almost anything can be spiritual – and he means literally a rock. He refers to the legend about a rock that followed the Israelites through the desert and wherever they camped, that rock followed them and gushed out water. That rock was a spiritual rock and it was super-real, more rock than any other rock.

The opposition between spirit and body actually comes from a misunderstanding of biblical language. The Bible opposes spirit and flesh, that is the only appropriate opposition in the Bible. Most unfortunately flesh got confused with body, but they are totally different things.

The point of the opposition between spirit and flesh is based on an everyday experience. Spirit was 'breath' and as long as something was breathing, it was alive. What made it alive was breath, so breath stood for life. When the breath went out, all that was left was a lump of meat. That's flesh. And particularly in the near East in the time before refrigeration, it very soon started smelling and crawling.

The whole idea of flesh has nothing to do with body or matter; it has to do with decay. Spirit means life-giving and alive, and flesh means death-bound, decaying, that which undoes itself. Therefore when Paul lists the sins of the flesh, very few of them have anything to do with the body. They are things like back-biting, envy and greed. That's decay: the decay of a society, the decay of a community. So when you read 'flesh', think of decay, and when you read 'spirit' think of life.

The spiritual work of our time is the task of making things alive, of rerooting – because if something is cut off from its roots, it will sooner or later die. That's the image of flesh – something that's cut off from its life, its roots.

(Brother David, Resurgence 119, November 1986)

The Pope celebrates Mass in Dublin

The *World Christian Encylopedia* (1982) states that there are around 20 800 distinct **denominations** (branches) in Christianity. All these denominations belong to much larger groups or 'families'. If we look at unit 5, we can see how the Church became split into three great families. The chart opposite shows the major differences between these families.

In the next few units we shall be looking at these great families.

The Roman Catholic Church

The Roman Catholic Church believes itself, historically and in its teachings, to be in continuity with the first disciples. The Church holds that God's teachings have been safeguarded and made authentic by the authority of the Church. This authority is exercised especially by the bishops of the local churches, who are still in harmony with the Bishop of Rome (the Pope). Roman Catholics believe that the Pope is the successor of Peter, the disciple (see unit 4). The Pope has special authority and Roman Catholics believe that he is **infallible** (without error) when he speaks to and in the name of the Church, on questions of faith or morals.

In order to help us understand some of the main beliefs and teachings of the Roman Catholic Church here are some extracts from the **catechism**. The catechism is a series of questions and answers used by the Church to help people understand the beliefs and teachings of the Church.

The Catechism

Question	Answer
Who is Jesus?	Jesus is the eternal Son of God who became truly and completely human in the womb of Mary while remaining truly and completely divine. The mystery of the true humanity and true divinity of Jesus is called the Incarnation.
Are Father, Son and Holy Spirit three Gods?	Father, Son and Holy Spirit are not three Gods, but three who are distinct from each other by their relationship with each other within the one Godhead. This mystery of the three who are one God is called the Trinity.
What is a sacrament?	A sacrament is a sacred sign by which we worship God, his love is revealed to us and his saving work accomplished in us.
What is the greatest sacrament?	The greatest sacrament of the church is the Eucharist (see unit 47).
What happens to the bread and wine in the celebration of the Eucharist?	By the power of the Holy Spirit the bread and wine cease to be bread and wine and become the body and blood of Christ himself really present to us.
What rules has the Church made for its members?	The main rules are to attend Mass on Sundays and certain major feasts; to follow the local regulations concerning penance on Ash Wednesday, Good Friday and other Fridays; to celebrate the Sacrament of Penance once a year if they have committed grave sin and to receive Communion during the Easter season; to contribute financially to the upkeep of the Church and its almsgiving.

(Roman Catholic Catechism, Catholic Truth Society)

	The Roman Catholic Church	The Orthodox Churches	The Reformed or Protestant Churches and Groups
What are they?	All Christians who acknowledge and accept the authority of the Pope (the Bishop of Rome). There are Catholic groups which are non-Roman, e.g. the Maronites of Lebanon.	A group of national or regional churches sometimes called 'eastern' Orthodox which originally accepted the leadership of the Patriarch of Constantinople. There are fifteen Orthodox Churches, including the Russian, Greek and Rumanian Orthodox Churches.	All Christian groups who base their beliefs and practices on the Reformation. They include Baptists, United Reformed Church, Methodists, Quakers, Lutherans, etc.
How are they organized?	The Pope is the Head and under him are cardinals, archbishops, priests. There are no separate branches but the Church does have 'orders' of monks and nuns.	Each Church is self-governing and independent and run by its own Patriarch. Under him there are bishops and priests. They have monks and nuns but they do not have separate 'orders'.	Each denomination has its own local, national (and sometimes international) organization. Most belong to the World Council of Churches (see unit 28).
What things do they stress?	• The authority of the Pope; • To be the one true Church; • The seven sacraments (see unit 46) of which the Mass is the central point.	• They have the true faith, beliefs and practices handed down by Jesus to his Apostles.	• The importance of the Bible, not the traditions of any Church; • The authority of the Bible does not require the Church to interpret it.

FOR YOUR FOLDERS

▶ After reading the chart write a paragraph on each of the three great families.
▶ Write an article of about 100 words on the major differences between the families.
!▶ What problems do you think these differences may have caused in the past and may cause today?
▶ Write a letter to a friend who knows nothing about the Roman Catholic Church explaining something about it.

KEY WORDS

Infallible – without error.
Catechism – a series of questions and answers used for instruction by the Roman Catholic Church.

The Second Vatican Council. Over 2000 bishops from all over the world attended

For many years the Roman Catholic Church altered very little in its organization, its beliefs and its attitude towards the other Christian Churches. However, in recent times, while still insisting on the truth of its traditional teachings, the Roman Catholic Church has begun to change its outlook on the world. These changes were set in motion by a seventy-six-year-old Italian Pope called Angelo Roncalli, who in 1958 became Pope John XXIII.

In 1962 Pope John XXIII called a Council of Roman Catholic Churchmen from all over the world to meet at the Vatican. This assembly of 2600 bishops, cardinals, abbots and heads of religious orders was called the Second Vatican Council. The First Vatican Council had been in 1869. The aim of the Council was to try to bring the Church up to date and make it more aware of the issues facing people in the

twentieth century. Before the Council, Pope John XXIII had set up the Vatican Secretariat for promoting Christian unity – a committee that looked at the relationship between the Roman Catholic Church and other churches.

When John XXIII died in 1963 his successor Pope Paul VI continued the work of the Council.

Why was the Second Vatican Council so important?

- For the first time the Roman Catholic Church began to acknowledge and listen to the other Christian Churches. A greater atmosphere of tolerance and trust was created. Religious intolerance and the religious persecutions of the past were condemned.

- Before the Council, worship was carried out in Latin. Millions of people never really understood what was being said. After the Council, worship was in the vernacular (i.e. the acutal language of the people).
- There was less Church censorship of reading material and teachers in schools had more freedom.
- The Church described belief as 'the pilgrim people of God'. This was a new emphasis underlining the importance of every believer, and seeing the followers of Jesus as being 'on the way together'.
- The problems facing people were looked at seriously. The Council called for the abolition of nuclear weapons; an end to the arms trade; a fairer distribution of the world's resources; a renewed struggle against racism; a greater understanding of the communist world.
- A more tolerant attitude was adopted towards other world religions.

However, many of the Church's teachings remained the same:
- Papal infallibility was confirmed. (Infallible means without error.)
- Beliefs about the Virgin Mary remained the same.
- Artificial forms of contraception were condemned.
- Abortion was 'an evil that poisoned society'.

TALKING POINTS FROM THE COUNCIL

- 'We must not remain indifferent to those communities whose citizens suffer from poverty, misery and hunger.'
- 'The arms race should cease . . . nuclear weapons should be banned.'
- 'Virginity must be regarded as a gift from God.'
- 'From the moment of conception life must be guarded with the greatest care.'
- All who are baptized have a right to be honoured as Christians.'

TALKING POINTS ABOUT THE COUNCIL

- 'So much has happened so quickly that there is uncertainty and confusion in many areas. Time alone will tell which way the Roman Catholic Church will go – but one thing is certain – it will not be back to the period before Vatican II.'
  (Lane, *Lion Concise Book of Christian Thought,* Lion 1984)
- 'If a man tried to compress into one sentence what the Council had done, he could say with confidence that it had further reinforced the already great authority of the Pope.'
  (*London Tablet*, 11 December 1965)

FOR YOUR FOLDERS

- ▶ What changes did the Second Vatican Council bring about?
- ▶ What teachings remained the same?
- ▶ What is papal infallibility? Why might some non-Catholics see this as causing problems for Church unity?
- ▶ Why do you think the Second Vatican Council is seen by many as being so important?
- ! ▶ What are your views on abortion and contraception?
- ▶ Imagine you are a newspaper reporter at the Council. Write an article about what you consider to be the most important aspects of the Council. The article should be about 200 words long.

23 THE ORTHODOX CHURCHES

Today there are an estimated 150 million Orthodox Christians in the world. There are two families, often called 'Eastern' and 'Oriental'. The Eastern family is the larger and consists of about twenty Churches including the Russian, Romanian, Bulgarian and Serbian Orthodox Churches and the Church of Greece. The overall leader of this Church is the Ecumenical Patriarch of Constantinople, All Holiness Dmitrios, who is based in Istanbul, Turkey. The smaller but older family, the Oriental Orthodox Church, has five Churches.

REFLECTION

'The Orthodox Church derives her teaching from two sources: Holy Scripture and Sacred Tradition. These two sources are of equal value. We believe that God is One in substance, We believe in the **Trinity**, worshipping One God in Trinity, and Trinity in Unity. Creation is the work of the Blessed Trinity. The World is not self-created, neither has it existed from eternity, but it is the product of the wisdom, the power and the will of the One God in Trinity. God the Father is the prime cause of creation and God the Son and God the Holy Spirit took part in creation. We believe that Our Lord Jesus Christ is truly God. He is Jesus, that is Saviour and Christ, the Lord's Anointed. He is also truly man like us in every respect except sin.

The **Church** is the holy institution founded by our Lord Jesus Christ for the salvation of men. It is divided into the clergy and laity. The clergy trace their descent from the **Apostles**. The Church is one, because our Lord Jesus Christ founded not many, but only one Church; holy because her aim, the salvation of her members through the Sacraments, is holy; catholic because she is above local limitations; and apostolic because she was "built upon the foundation of the Apostles, Jesus Christ Himself being the cornerstone". (Ephesians 2:20) The Head of the Church is our Lord, Jesus Christ.

We recognize the seven **sacraments**: Baptism, Chrismation, Holy Eucharist, Ordination, Marriage, Confession and Holy Unction ("anointing of the sick"). Baptism is the door through which one enters the Church; Confirmation is the completion of Baptism. In the Sacrament of the Holy Eucharist, with the bread and wine, we partake of the very Body and the very Blood of our Lord Jesus Christ for remissions of sins and eternal life. Our Lord is present in the Holy Eucharist. In the sacrament of Confession, Jesus Christ, the founder of the sacrament, through the confessor, forgives the sins committed after Baptism by the person who confesses his sins and sincerely repents of them. In the sacrament of Ordination, through prayer and the laying on of hands by a bishop, divine **grace** comes down on the ordained. In the sacrament of Marriage, divine grace sanctifies the union of husband and wife. In the sacrament of the Holy Unction the sick person is anointed with sanctified oil and divine grace heals his bodily and spiritual ills.

Further we honour the saints and we ask their intercession with God, but we adore and worship God, the Father and the Son and the Holy Spirit. Of all Saints we honour exceedingly the Mother of our Lord because of the grace and the call which she received from God. We venerate the sacred **icons** and relics. Yet this veneration, does not relate to the sacred images as such, but to the persons whom they represent.'

(Summarized from Orthodox News 4:1, September 1986)

Procession by Orthodox Christians

'Of all saints we honour exceedingly the mother of our Lord'

TALKING POINT

- 'We know that our life is temporary, and we had better live with Christ and offer ourselves, and have true life in him. . . . The pressures of life have brought us that really deep life of close relation with God.' (Pope Shenouda III, Leader of the Egyptian Coptic Church)

FOR YOUR FOLDERS

After reading this unit, answer the following questions about the Orthodox Christians:

- ▶ Where do they derive their teachings from?
- ▶ What do they believe about creation, the Church and the Eucharist?
- ▶ What are the seven sacraments?
- ▶ Write a sentence about each of the seven sacraments.
- ▶ Which saint do they 'honour exceedingly'?
- ▶ What is an icon?
- ▶ Write an essay called 'The central beliefs of Orthodox Christians'.

24 THE PROTESTANT CHURCHES

As we have seen in unit 5, the Protestant Churches grew from the Reformation in the sixteenth century. In this unit we shall be looking at some of the main characteristics of the most important Protestant Churches.

The Lutheran Church

The Lutheran Church is found mainly in the German-speaking countries, Scandinavia and North America. There are about 70 million Lutherans in the world today and they trace their origins back to the teachings of the German monk, Martin Luther (1483–1546). They stress Luther's ideas, especially the idea of 'justification by faith' which Luther defined as 'having true faith that Christ is your saviour, then at once you will have a gracious God'. In their worship they emphasize preaching, the sacraments, Bible readings and **hymn** singing and they allow women to become **priests**.

The Calvinist Churches

The Calvinist or Reformed Churches are found in Europe, North America and South Africa. They take their name from the French reformer John Calvin (1509–1564). There are three types of leader at a local level: the minister, the elder and the deacon. Because the elder (or 'Presbyter') is the key figure in the structure, many Reformed Churches in English-speaking countries call themselves Presbyterian. The national Church of Scotland is Presbyterian.

The Free Churches

From the English-speaking churches of the seventeenth and eighteenth centuries came a number of churches now known as the Free Churches or Non-conformist Churches. The best known include the Baptists, the Methodists, the Pentecostal Churches, the Salvation Army and the Society of Friends (sometimes known as 'Quakers').

THE BAPTISTS

There are some 32 million Baptists world-wide. The main characteristics of the Baptist Churches are:
- 'the priesthood of believers' – all members fully participate in every aspect of the life of the Church.
- 'Believers' **baptism**' – only people who are able to understand and accept the Christian faith, and who can explain their own personal decision to follow Jesus Christ, are baptized (see unit 46).

THE METHODISTS

The founders of Methodism were two eighteenth-century Anglican clergymen, John Wesley (1703–1791) and Charles Wesley (1707–1788). Methodists keep their worship simple. It is made up of hymn singing, prayers, Bible readings and a sermon. Except for Holy Communion they rarely use a service book. Hymn singing plays an important part of Methodism. The Wesleys, who wrote some of the finest hymns in the Christian religion, wanted to 'inject some life into services'. The first words in the Methodist hymn book state, 'Methodism was born in song'.

Hymn singing plays an important part in Methodist worship

THE PENTECOSTAL CHURCHES

(See unit 9)

THE SALVATION ARMY

The Salvation Army was founded by William Booth (1829–1912), a Methodist minister who worked in the slums of Victorian England. The movement is built on military lines. The minister is an 'officer', the members are 'soldiers', and they all wear uniforms. The place where they meet for worship is called a 'Citadel'. The Salvation Army works all over the world among the poor and underprivileged. Music is a very important part of the Army's worship, and every service or open air meeting is filled with the sounds of brass bands, hand clapping and the singing of 'songs' (hymns). There is no set form of worship and the leader of a meeting has almost complete freedom to plan it as he or she wishes.

The Society of Friends ('Quakers')

'Quaker' was the nickname given to the founder of the Society of Friends, George Fox (1624–1691), by a judge whom he told to 'quake and fear at the word'. Quakers' worship is extremely simple and they reject all ceremony. They base their religion on the belief that God speaks directly to the heart of everyone. They have no creed, sacraments, ordained ministry, ordered services or sacred buildings. In their services silence is important, with people speaking if they feel moved to do so.

Quakers have always worked in many areas to make the world a better place. They are pacifists (see Unit 71) and refuse to resort to the use of violence. Their Peace Testimony has been an inspiration to many Christians through the ages:

PEACE TESTIMONY OF THE SOCIETY OF FRIENDS

We utterly deny all outward wars and strife, and fightings with outward weapons, for any end, or under any pretence whatever; this is our testimony to the whole world. The Spirit of Christ by which we are guided is not changeable, so as once to command us from a thing as evil, and again to move unto it; and we certainly know, and testify to the world, that the Spirit of Christ which leads us into all truth, will never move us to fight and war against any man with outward weapons, neither for the kingdom of Christ, nor for the kingdoms of the world.

(from *A Declaration from the Harmless and Innocent People of God, called Quakers*, presented to Charles II, 1660)

FOR YOUR FOLDERS

► Explain the following words and phrases: Protestant; justification by faith; Presbyter; Free Churches; Citadel; priesthood of all believers; believers' baptism; Quaker.
► Write a few sentences about the main characteristics of the different groups you've looked at in this unit, and about Martin Luther; John Calvin; the Wesleys; William Booth; George Fox.

25 THE ANGLICAN CHURCH

A procession in Canterbury Cathedral, the historic centre of the Anglican communion

The Church of England (sometimes called the **Anglican** Church) began in England, but today it is found all over the world. In England, the Church of England is often called the 'established Church'. Since it separated from the Church of Rome, in the sixteenth century, the King or Queen of England has been its head. This means that the Church of England is closely linked with many aspects of life in England. Bishops of the Church are entitled to sit in the House of Lords and take part in the government of the country. This link with the state does not occur in other countries, nor does it occur in Wales, Scotland or Ireland.

The Anglican Church is not really a Protestant Church, indeed some Anglicans would say that it is part of the 'Catholic' Church (not the Roman Catholic Church). Although some Anglican Churches retain many Roman Catholic traditions in their beliefs and practices, some Churches are closer to the Protestant tradition.

> *'At its best – this is the ideal . . . the Anglican Church . . . tries to hold together the more Catholic traditions; the evangelical emphasis on the Bible and personal conversion and openness to new ideas.'*
> (Donald Coggan, formerly Archbishop of Canterbury)

Because of this diversity it is difficult to say exactly what the Anglican Church is. However, at the Lambeth Conference in 1920, emphasis was put on the following:

- The Holy Scriptures contain everything necessary for salvation.
- The Apostles' Creed and the Nicene Creed express Christian faith.
- The two sacraments of Baptism and the Lord's Supper are celebrated.
- 'The historic episcopate' (i.e. the line of bishops in a carefully maintained succession) is preserved. The bishops should carry out their duties according to the varying needs of the nations and peoples called by God.

Today the Church of England has about 18 000 churches, most of them easily distinguished by the square tower or lofty spire outside and the long nave leading to the altar inside.

A worldwide Church

During the eighteenth and nineteenth centuries the Church of England expanded rapidly throughout the world. This was due to the expanding British Empire, and the activity of the missionary societies. The Anglican Churches are found in countries which were once colonies but now have independence, e.g. Australia, Canada, West Indies. They are also to be found throughout Asia, Africa and Latin America. Although many of these Churches are independent they are linked to England; for instance every ten years the Churches will meet at the Lambeth Conference under the presidency of the Archbishop of Canterbury. All the independent Anglican Churches see the Archbishop of Canterbury as being their leader. The Lambeth Conference (so called because the Archbishop's residence is at Lambeth Palace in London) helps to keep unity within the different Churches. The Book of Common Prayer also helps keep a sense of unity. This is used in all Anglican services worldwide. It was first used in the sixteenth century, and some Churches still use the original version. However, many Churches now use modern versions. The Book of Common Prayer ensures that in Churches all over the world there are certain central ingredients (e.g. hymns, psalms, confessional prayers, sermons, etc.) that are common to all Anglican services. All Churches have certain preferences about ways of worship but the outline of the service is familiar all over the world.

The Church at Work

The Church of England is concerned about the type of society we live in. It has many organizations concerned with helping the poor, helpless and underprivileged members of society. Two such organizations are:

- **The Children's Society** which runs adoption agencies, schools and nurseries for disabled children, gypsy playgroups, hostels for single mothers and their babies, etc. as well as promoting the welfare of deprived children in society.
- **The Church Army** made up of about 150 'officers' who help the aged, run housing schemes for the homeless, run hostels, work with prisoners, etc.

Prayers, psalms, canticles and hymns play an important part of Anglican Church services. Here is the Benedicte Omnia Opera, one of the most beautiful canticles used in the services:

1   *O all ye works of the Lord, bless ye the Lord: praise him, and magnify him for ever.*

2   *O ye angels of the Lord, bless ye the Lord: praise him, and magnify him for ever.*

3   *O ye heavens, bless ye the Lord:*
O ye waters that be above the firmament, bless ye the Lord:
O all ye powers of the Lord, bless ye the Lord:
    praise him and magnify him for ever.

4   *O ye sun and moon, bless ye the Lord:*
O ye stars of heaven, bless ye the Lord:
O ye showers and dew, bless ye the Lord:
    praise him, and magnify him for ever.

5   *O ye winds of God, bless ye the Lord:*
O ye fire and heat, bless ye the Lord:
O ye winter and summer, bless ye the Lord:
    praise him, and magnify him for ever.

6   *O ye dews and frosts, bless ye the Lord:*
O ye frost and cold, bless ye the Lord:
O ye ice and snow, bless ye the Lord:
    praise him, and magnify him for ever.

7   *O ye nights and days, bless ye the Lord:*
O ye light and darkness, bless ye the Lord:
O ye lightnings and clouds, bless ye the Lord:
    praise him, and magnify him for ever.

8   *O let the earth bless the Lord:*
O ye mountains and hills, bless ye the Lord:
O all ye green things upon the earth, bless ye the Lord:
    praise him, and magnify him for ever.

9   *O ye wells, bless ye the Lord:*
O ye seas and floods, bless ye the Lord:
O ye whales and all that move in the waters, bless ye the Lord:
    praise him, and magnify him for ever.

10   *O all ye fowls of the air, bless ye the Lord:*
O all ye beasts and cattle, bless ye the Lord:
O ye children of men, bless ye the Lord:
    praise him, and magnify him for ever.

11   *O let Israel bless the Lord:*
O ye priests of the Lord, bless ye the Lord:
O ye servants of the Lord, bless ye the Lord:
    praise him, and magnify him for ever.

12   *O ye spirits and souls of the righteous, bless ye the Lord:*
O ye holy and humble men of heart, bless ye the Lord:
O Ananias, Azarias, and Misael, bless ye the Lord:
    praise him, and magnify him for ever.
Glory be to the Father, and to the Son: and to the Holy Spirit;
As it was in the beginning, is now, and ever shall be: world without end. Amen.

FOR YOUR FOLDERS

▶ Why is the Church of England often called the 'established Church'?

▶ Why do you think the Anglican Church has been called 'the middle way'?

▶ Which event and which book have helped keep a sense of unity within the Anglican Church?

▶ It is estimated that about three per cent of the total population of England attend an Anglican church, yet nearly fifty per cent of children are baptized in one. Do you think England can be called a 'Christian society'?

▶ In the last few units you have studied the 'three great families'. Write an article about them called 'A family divided yet together'.

26 THE EVANGELICALS

Evangelical Christians are among the fastest growing groups in Christianity today. It has been estimated that one in six (or about 270 million) of the world's Christians are evangelicals. The word 'evangelical' is defined as 'certain Christian churches which believe in the importance of religious teaching, of faith and of studying the Bible, rather than in ceremonies' (*Longman's Dictionary of Contemporary English*), and 'churches or individuals who present the "good news" with a view to the conversion of hearers to their faith' (*A Dictionary of RE*, Longman).

Basically, evangelical Christians stress:
- the Bible is the inspired word of God;
- the need for a personal relationship with Jesus Christ through 'conversion' and a 'new birth';
- their commitment to convert others.

The Charismatic Movement

In the various Christian denominations, there are sometimes groups and congregations who exhibit an uninhibited joy about their faith (see photograph). Worshippers often clap their hands, raise their hands or lead the prayers. This movement first emerged in California in the USA in the 1960s and became known as the **Charismatic Movement**. The word 'charismatic' comes from a Greek word meaning 'gifts', referring to the special powers Christians believe are given by the Holy Spirit. These gifts include healing, prophecy and speaking in tongues (see unit 4). The Charismatic Movement (sometimes called 'The Renewal') has influenced many Christians of all denominations.

House churches

In Britain a fairly new phenomenon has appeared on the Christian scene. This is 'house churches'. Originally, as the name suggests, people would worship in one another's houses. Today, as the movement has grown, the worshippers may meet in halls, old cinemas, rented school buildings, etc. In the last few years purpose-built centres have sprung up.

House churches originated among many Christians who felt that traditional places of worship had become too formal, inflexible and unfriendly. They looked for a less formal and more friendly and personal environment.

Waiting for the rapture

Fundamentalist Christianity offers a clear prescription for divine worship and human action. And in the process it injects a lot of ideology into its theology. Brian Aitkins sums up the principles of fundamentalist belief.

It is extremely difficult to separate fundamentalism's religious agenda from its political agenda. Like so much of American Christianity, it is really kind of a 'civil religion', where Christian ideas are wed to traditional American values – and in this case with hawkish values. Fundamentalism presents us with a vision which is part theology and part ideology.

At the centre of this vision is God's Holy Word, the Bible. It was dictated to 'man' by God and expresses God's will in every verse, word and comma. The Bible is essentially 'a great code' containing clear-cut rules and regulations which cover every sphere of life. In practice, however fundamentalism also seems to venerate civil laws and traditional American virtues such as hard work, honesty and sobriety. So the great code for fundamentalists involves both the Bible and the law of the land. And fundamentalism's message is clear: if people wish to remain secure and holy in a world of rapid change and constant temptation, they must scrupulously follow the great code.

The fundamentalist god is one of power and judgement. His love and blessing comes only to those who give him absolute obedience. This theology of power is linked directly to an ideology of power. God has structured power and authority into the fabric of society. Politicians are appointed by God to rule society, husbands are called to rule their wives, fathers their children, and bosses their employees. For fundamentalists, to question any authority is to question God and God's system of power. The fundamentalist view of power preserves a social order which has given adult males an enormous amount of control over women and children.

Fundamentalism sees human history as a battleground. As God battles with Satan and his

Moved by the Spirit: A young believer in a moment of ecstasy.

legions, so the righteous in this world must do battles with demonic forces. For fundamentalism the present guise of the demonic is 'secular humanism', which fundamentalist polemicist Tim LaHaye defines as combining atheism, amoralism, a belief in evolution and a socialist one world view. For LaHaye secular humanism is a religion which has infiltrated every sphere of American life. Much of the New Right's attempt to censor pornography, preserve the traditional nuclear family and have the 'creationist' view taught in schools comes out of fundamentalism's compulsion to combat the sinister forces embodied in secular humanism.

(New Internationalist)

FOR YOUR FOLDERS

▶ Look at the photograph. What aspects of charismatic worship can you describe in them?

▶ Explain why house churches have become popular.

▶ What do evangelical Christians stress?

▶ After reading the above article, explain some of the main beliefs of American fundamentalist Christians.

▶ *'Fundamentalism presents us with a vision which is part theology and part ideology.'* What do you think this means? What is this ideology? What do you think about it?

Christianity is a world religion. It has influenced and been influenced by cultures all over the world, and this can be clearly seen in the huge continent of Africa. Africa is a continent of great diversity. The conditions, beliefs and practices in Africa are as varied as the continent itself. Christianity is not a new phenomenon in Africa. The Ethiopian Othodox Church was founded in the fourth century CE and the Coptic Orthodox Church was traditionally founded by St Mark in the first century CE.

As European missionaries worked in Africa, they imported their own European style of Christianity. They brought with them European styles of buildings, dress, music, beliefs and values. Seldom did they make any real or sustained effort to understand or even consider traditional African religions which were thousands of years old and contained a great wealth of ideas and practices. This ignorance by many missionaries often led to the Africans being treated very badly, and helped to fuel such evils as the slave trade, which resulted in eight million people being torn away from their land and shipped to places like America.

However, in the twentieth century, as more African countries gained political independence, Christianity in Africa began to change. Many African Churches began to break away from the patterns and ideas that they had received from the missionaries. They remained as Christians, but began to use African ideas and patterns to express their beliefs and faith. These Churches have become known as the Independent African Churches and their beliefs and practices vary tremendously throughout Africa.

The Christian religion is rapidly expanding in Africa.

'In 1900 9% of Africans considered themselves to be Christians. By the mid 1980s, 44% of Africans considered themselves to be Christians and by the year 2000 it is estimated that this figure will be nearing 49%.'
(World Christian Encyclopedia, Lion, 1985)

Some characteristics

Many African Independent Churches have grown by exploiting and using traditional African dances, music, story-telling, symbols and rituals. Christian themes are expressed in truly African ways through ancient African customs, and some Churches include African ideas about worshipping ancestors. For some Churches Jesus Christ is 'the light' who disperses the evil powers of darkness, while for others he is the 'giver of life' and 'the healer'. Some of the most popular types of Church are the 'prophet healing' Churches. The founders and leaders of these Churches are called 'prophets', who claim to have received a vision from God who empowered them to heal in his name.

Many of these Churches grew out of a response of the failure of missionaries to relate Christianity to the traditional African view of the world. Often the missionaries condemned the traditional African way of life. They wanted to transform Africans into 'black Europeans'. For example, until relatively recently, African Christians had to be baptized with Christian names. An African name which might mean 'God is with me' was unacceptable because it was African.

The Yoruba

The Yoruba tribe of Nigeria, consisting of over ten million people, have many prophet healing Churches. In this reflection some of the practices and beliefs are explained.

Africa is a continent of ancient cultures and religions

REFLECTION

'The prophet will be garbed in his prayer gown. Shouting and gesturing his message in a strong rhythm to the circle of onlookers he will suddenly break into song. A powerful beat is maintained and a dance step is taken up. The song is a simple lyric and the people join in. This will be followed by a prayer in which God is addressed with vigour and almost hypnotic repetitiveness. The onlookers respond as they share in the petitions for God's help against witchcraft, his victory over sin, his guidance over their lives and blessings for their children. If the visitor follows the prophet back to the church there may be people already there – some lying on mats on the floor, others sitting on plain wooden benches. They are sick people living in the sanctuary in order to absorb its holiness and power, which is believed to have healing qualities. A client asks the prophet to pray for him. The prophet places his hand on the client's head and launches into a powerful prayer for God's help. These prophet healing Churches are called "Aladura" which means "owner of prayer" and these prophets certainly give a feeling of God's power and holiness.

The Sunday service is only one of a number of services, during the week. Early every morning the day begins with prayer and singing; every workday is brought to a close the same way. One or more mornings during the week the prophet will have "clinic" services which are especially directed to healing. Some Aladura churches have weekly "watch-night" services. These occur on Saturday beginning late in the evening and continuing until the Holy Spirit, who is summoned to come into the congregation, leaves the participants sweating, exhausted, but joyful with the confidence that God has spoken directly to them through the revelations of the people chosen by him that evening. Adding to their joy is their confidence that witches have been directly confronted during their hours of terrible activity by the power of the living God and his son Jesus, and banished from their lives no more to cause sickness, misfortune or death.

Periodically the enthusiasm of the watch-night service is reconstructed during a series of weekly early evening services called revivals which are meant to stir the hearts of the faithful and to exhibit the power of God to those people who are not members of the congregation.'

(Robert C. Mitchell 'African Primal Religions', in D. K. Swearer (ed.), Major World Religion Series, Tabor Publishing 1977)

TALKING POINT

- 'Africa has been and still is exploited by the western world. We were led to believe that Africa had things to learn from us. We were wrong. We must learn from Africa – her cultures, traditions and religions are steeped in ancient knowledge, beauty and wisdom. We must wake up and learn from Africa because our culture and quality of life is asleep.'

FOR YOUR FOLDERS

▶ After reading this unit try to explain in an article of about 200 words what the Independent Churches in Africa are all about, i.e. how and why they arose, what they are trying to do and some of their beliefs and practices.

KEY IDEA

African theology is concerned to express the Christian gospel against an African cultural background, and to take as positive attitude as possible to African traditions while remaining true to the Gospels.

Young Christians from many denominations take part in a service in Taizé

'I have other sheep, that are not of this fold; I must bring them also, and they will heed my voice. So there shall be one flock, one shepherd.'

(John 10:16)

The history of the Christian Church has often been one of conflict, bloodshed and persecution. The world's Christians are divided into three main groups: Catholic, Orthodox and Protestant Christians.

However, the twentieth century has seen a great deal of work to heal these divisions and conflicts and attempts are being made to produce a far greater unity among the Christian Churches.

A movement called the Ecumenical Movement has emerged. The word **ecumenical** comes from the Greek 'oikoumene' which means the whole inhabited world, and refers to unity among Christians in the world.

In this unit we shall be looking at some of this work. It will be useful if you refer to other units, so that you can begin to get an overall picture of the Ecumenical Movement.

What is the Ecumenical Movement?

'The reason for the existence of the Ecumenical Movement was a missionary one. Divisions among Christians hindered the Churches' efforts to spread the Gospel. This does not mean that the movement pushes for a "sameness" among Christians which would destroy what is distinctive and valuable in each Christian tradition; but it does call on Christians to co-operate in worship and service as far as conscience allows and to take all possible steps to grow in understanding of others. A cynic might say that the Churches are coming together to fight for survival, at a time when their influence and numbers are declining. But it is also the case that many exciting and creative things are happening at all levels of the Church.'
(Adapted from Dr Lorna Brockett, *The Ecumenical Movement*, CEM 1985)

The World Council of Churches

An organization that has had a great influence on the ecumenical movement is the World Council of Churches (see unit 28). This was founded in Amsterdam in 1948. With representatives from the Orthodox and Protestant Churches it spearheads and promotes united Christian action throughout the world. As well as dealing with religious themes it also looks at current world problems, like racism, the arms trade, human rights and world poverty. Critics of the WCC have accused it of being too much concerned with political issues rather than with the Gospel, but for some Christians today, working for peace and justice is seen as part of the following of Jesus Christ. The WCC claims to represent over 400 million Christians. It does not claim to be a sort of 'super-Church', but rather a fellowship of Churches. The Roman Catholic Church is not a member of the WCC although some Catholic representatives have taken part in some activities.

The Pan-Orthdox Conference

This was set up by the Orthodox Church in 1961 and its main aim is to enter into friendly discussions – aimed at promoting unity – with all non-Orthodox Christians.

The Second Vatican Council

(1962–1965, see unit 22.) During the first half of the twentieth century the Roman Catholic Church saw itself as the one true Church, and saw Christain unity in terms of the return of separated Christians to the 'true Church in Rome'. However, the Second Vatican Council saw the beginning of changing attitudes towards other Christians.

> 'The Council recognized the bonds of unity which exist between the Roman Catholic and other Churches, and by the tone of respect and affection in which it speaks of other Christians. It rejects aggressive controversy and moves towards a genuine search for mutual understanding.'
> (Dr Lorna Brockett, *The Ecumenical Movement*, CEM 1985)

Since the Council, a growing relationship between the Protestant and Catholic Churches has emerged and has been strengthened by meetings between successive Popes and Archbishops. There are still controversial areas like the Pope's authority, ordination of women, married priests and the Eucharist, but now debate and discussion is beginning to take the place of aggressive argument between the Churches.

Communities

We can also see the effects of the Ecumenical Movement in certain communities which are trying to promote a more ecumenical approach. These include communities at Corrymeela (see unit 31), Taizé and Iona (see unit 30).

FOR YOUR FOLDERS

▶ Write a sentence about the following words and phrases: ecumenical; unity; WCC; Second Vatican Council.

▶ *'Church attendances falling'.* How could some people argue that the Ecumenical Movement grew because of fears about the survival of the Church?

▶ What problems does the Ecumenical Movement still face?

▶ *'The road ahead for Christian unity is long and hard, yet the rewards for its achievement would be immense.'*
(David Pringle)
What do you think these rewards might be?

TALKING POINT

● 'The ecumenical dialogue is today anything but the speciality of a few starry-eyed peaceniks. For the first time in history it has now taken on the character of an urgent desire for world politics. It can help to make our earth more livable, by making it more peaceful and reconciled.'
(Hans Küng, Christianity and the World Religions, Collins 1987)

REFLECTION

. . . We are filled with praise to God for the grace given to us since our last meeting. In many places churches have grown in numbers and depth of commitment. We rejoice in courage and faith shown in adversity. We are humbled by those newly called to be martyrs. The Holy Spirit has poured out these and many other gifts, so that we meet with thanksgiving.

This meeting comes in a succession which began at Amsterdam in 1948 with the commitment to stay together. Since then we have been called to grow together and to struggle together. Here under the theme "Jesus Christ, the Life of the World" we are called to live together . . .

We hear the cries of millions who face a daily struggle for survival, who are crushed by military power or the propaganda of the powerful. We see the camps of refugees and the tears of all who suffer inhuman loss. We sense the fear of rich groups and nations and the hopelessness of many in the world rich in things who live in great emptiness of spirit. There is a great divide between North and South, between East and West. Our world – God's world – has to choose between "life and death, blessing and curse" . . .

The misery and chaos of the world result from the rejection of God's design for us. Constantly, in public and private, fellowship is broken, life is mutilated and we live alone. In the life of Jesus we meet the very life of God, face to face. He experienced our life, our birth and childhood, our tiredness, our laughter and tears. He shared food with the hungry, love with the rejected, healing with the sick, forgiveness with the penitent. . .

The division of the Church at central points of its life, our failure to witness with courage and imagination, our clinging to old prejudice, our share in the injustice of the world – all this tells us that we are disobedient. Yet God's graciousness amazes us, for we are still called to be God's people, the house of living stones built on Christ the foundation. One sign of this grace is the Ecumenical Movement in which no member or Church stands alone.

The Assembly therefore renews its commitment to Church unity. We take slow, stumbling steps on the way to the visible unity of the Church but we are sure the direction is essential to our faithfulness. . .

We renew our commitment to mission and evangelism. By this we mean that deep identification with others in which we can tell the good news that Jesus Christ, God and Saviour, is the Life of the World. We cannot impose faith by our eloquence. We can nourish it with patience and caring so that the Holy Spirit, God the Evangelist, may give us the words to speak. Our proclamation has to be translated into every language and culture. Whatever our context among people of living faith and no faith, we remember that God's love is for everyone, without exception. . .

We renew our commitment to justice and peace. Since Jesus Christ healed and challenged the whole of life, so we are called to serve the life of all. We see God's good gift battered by the powers of death. Injustice denies God's gifts of unity, sharing and responsibility. When nations, groups and systems hold the power of deciding other people's lives, they love that power. God's way is to share power, to give it to every person. . .

The arms race everywhere consumes great resources that are desperately needed to support human life. Those who threaten with military might are dealing in the politics of death. It is a time of crisis for us all. We stand in solidarity across the world to call persistently, in every forum, for a halt to the arms race. The life which is God's good gift must be guarded when national security becomes the excuse for arrogant militarism. The tree of peace has justice for its roots.

Life is given. We receive God's gift with constant thankfulness. . . We are astounded and surprised that the eternal purpose of God is persistently entrusted to ordinary people. That is the risk God takes. The forces of death are strong. The gift of life in Christ is stronger. We commit ourselves to live that life, with all its risks and joys, and therefore dare to cry, with all the host of heaven, "O death, where is your victory?' Christ is risen. He is risen indeed.'

(WCC 'One World', WCC Magazine)

The World Council of Churches (WCC) was formed in 1948.

'It is a fellowship of Churches which confess the Lord Jesus Christ as God and Saviour according to the Scriptures, and therefore seek to fulfil together their common calling to the glory of the One God, Father, Son and Holy Spirit.'

Apart from the Roman Catholic Church and some Evangelical Churches, all significant Christian Churches now belong to the WCC. Since 1961 the Roman Catholic Church has sent official observers to the general assemblies. There have been six major general assemblies: in Holland (1948), USA (1954), India (1961), Sweden (1968), Kenya (1975) and Canada (1983). These assemblies are attended by thousands of delegates from all over the world. They discuss a wide variety of issues.

The twentieth century has seen remarkable progress towards Christian unity. There have been few Church mergers, but there have been great changes in the attitudes of different Churches to one another. Most Churches recognize that they do not necessarily possess the whole truth and are more willing to learn from others.

The WCC has not been without troubles and controversy. For example, some Christians have argued that the WCC has become too 'political', whereas others believe that part of the Christian mission on earth is to become involved with political and social issues. Generally the WCC has three main areas of work:

- faith and witness – making people aware of the Christian message;
- justice and service – helping to promote peace and justice in the world;
- communication – promoting tolerance and knowledge globally.

FOR YOUR FOLDERS

Read the reflection and answer the following questions:
- ▶ Who are the millions who face 'a daily struggle for survival'?
- ▶ What is the 'Ecumenical Movement'?
- ▶ What do you think were the major concerns of this Assembly?
- ▶ What do you think are some of the major beliefs of the WCC?
- ▶ *'The misery and chaos of the world result from the rejection of God's design for us.'* Comment.

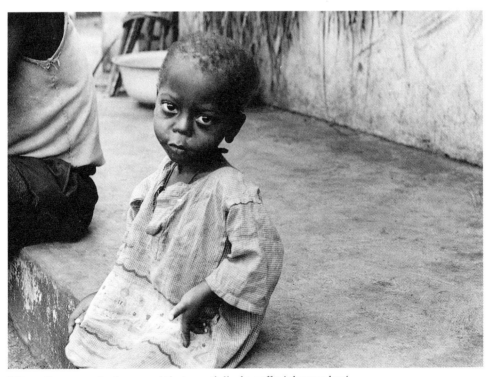

'We see the camps of refugees and the tears of all who suffer inhuman loss'

Taizé

'That Christ may grow in me, I must know my own weakness and that of my brothers. For them I will become all things to all, and even give my life, for Christ's sake and the Gospel's.'

(From the rule of the community)

These words are often spoken by the brothers of Taizé, a Christian community in a small village in France. The brothers, who come from all over the world themselves, work amongst the poor in places like Kenya, New York, Bangladesh and Japan.

The Taizé community was founded by a young student called Roger Schutz in 1940. He felt strongly that there was a need for a new kind of monasticism within the Protestant Church. The community of Taizé takes the traditional vows of poverty, chastity and obedience. The brothers provide for thousands of visitors every year and have their own printing press, co-operative farm and pottery. Taizé is particularly aware of the needs of young people and every year thousands of them from all over the world camp in the fields around the monastery, taking part in private and public worship, discussions and manual work.

This reflection gives an account of one person's experiences at Taizé:

REFLECTION

'The Church of Reconciliation rose in front of me . . . inside it was dark, cool and crowded. We sat on the carpeted floor. It was quiet; the brothers in robes knelt or sat in a wide line down the centre of the church. The service began. We sang, listened to Bible readings in several languages, prayed in even more languages; then a long period of silence, meditation. To sit on the floor – shoulder to shoulder – in silence – this was very powerful. I could feel the silence. After this, you could take communion, Roman Catholics on one side of the church, the rest on the other.'

'Lying on my bed, events of the day flashed by, as did the week. Talking and listening, caring and sharing, discussing what Christianity had to offer – and not only with Christians. What remains in my mind? – the weekly Easter perhaps! The pace quickens, the church is jam-packed on Fridays as the cross is laid flat on the floor, prayers are offered for persecuted Christians and for those who are prisoners of conscience. You may press your head to the cross as a sign to commit all that weighs you down to Christ.

It is sad to leave a place where one has felt at home. I had only really started to understand Taizé. It wasn't just the personality of Brother Roger, nor the brothers, nor the place, nor even all the people I had shared my life with for a week. In some way it was all of them rolled into one. To be part of something living, vital, enthusiastic and emotional is tremendous, for it makes you vital too. Perhaps the vitality in all of us is to be used for the benefits of the community.'

(Author's interview)

Iona

Iona is an island off the west coast of Scotland. It has been a holy place since St Columba went there in 563 CE. The community was founded by the Reverend George Macleod in 1938. Whilst working in the slum areas of Glasgow, Macleod had come to believe that many working people had lost touch with the Church. He wanted to form a community in which everyone from all walks of life could live, work and worship together. After years of hard work Macleod and others rebuilt the abbey on the island and the community grew. Today there are about 150 people. Over 1000 people a year visit the abbey and the youth camp. Members of the community keep half an hour for prayer every morning, give five per cent of their money to the community fund and try to live together by following the Christian ideal. This reflection gives an account of a visit made to Iona by a sixteen-year-old girl:

REFLECTION

'Iona struck me almost immediately as being a beautiful and special place. The light is so bright, the sea so wild and the weather so changeable. We were met from our small boat by two community members who took us to the restored abbey. After dinner we introduced ourselves – everyone was so friendly and we were given our little chores for the week.

During the week we had talks and discussions about all sorts of things, especially about world poverty and world peace. We learnt about how the work of Iona goes on in the slums of Glasgow and we felt the commitment of the people living on Iona. After a week there I felt rested both in body and mind. In a strange sort of way I felt that I had experienced a force greater than myself – I call this force God. I had also made friends for life because they had lived and shared this Iona experience with me.'

(Author's interview)

FOR YOUR FOLDERS

► Write a sentence about Roger Schutz and one about George Macleod.
► What do you think are the aims of the Taizé and Iona communities?
► Why did the person at Taizé describe his experience as 'vital and enthusiastic'?
► Note some of the similarities and differences between the two communities.

Brother Roger with young people in the Church of Reconciliation at Taizé

Since 1969 and the outbreak of unrest in Northern Ireland, few days have passed without our television screens or newspapers reporting some human tragedy. Northern Ireland has been torn apart by internal division and the religious conflict between Roman Catholics and Protestants is often said to be the root cause of this conflict. Whether this is true or not, in one part of Northern Ireland a religious community is trying in its own way to work for peace.

Corrymeela was founded in 1965 by Christians, Catholics and Protestants, who were aware of the deep divisions within Northern Ireland. The main site is at Ballycastle on the beautiful County Antrim coast.

The main aim of the community, which has 140 members and over 1000 'friends', is reconciliation. The Ballycastle centre provides a place where people from different traditions can meet and talk freely. In the course of the year, 8000 people from a wide variety of traditions and backgrounds visit Corrymeela. Each group is in residence for between two days and a week. They include families under stress, like families of prisoners; those bereaved in the violence; single-parent groups; those from areas of tension and social deprivation; school, youth and church groups; the unemployed; the disabled; senior citizens; group conferences on peace work and social, political and religious issues; the victims of violence.

An important part of the work at Corrymeela concerns trying to help young people to understand themselves, their relationships and their communities. The community at Corrymeela run what is known as a 'seed group'. This involves about twenty young people between the ages of eighteen and twenty-one, meeting every weekend for six months. The Reverend Douglas Baker, a worker at Corrymeela, explains the ideas of the seed group:

'Jesus uses the way seeds grow as a parable to help his followers understand how God's kingdom grows in the world. It is a powerful message of hope for all who in each generation long for the spread of God's kingdom and through their own lives seek to become tools through whom it is nurtured. The aims we have identified for the "seed groups" are:

- **reflecting** on all of the experiences and influences which have shaped who we are – on the issues and choices which confront us in terms of who we shall become;
- **understanding** ourselves and our relationships with others;
- **relating** the Christian faith to our own experience;
- **building** bridges of trust, understanding and personal friendship;
- **encouraging** the development of ideas for reconcilation.'

(Reverend Douglas Baker)

The word of God, the rule of law . . . cross purposes in a divided province

In 1980 a BBC film crew visited Corrymeela. They spent a weekend with two groups of youths who lived in areas next to each other but had never met. One group were Protestants from the Woodstock area of Belfast and the other were Catholics from the Short Strand area. Some of the youths had lost a friend or family member in the troubles and many had experienced violence. Here are some of their comments:

'I still don't like them – the Catholics. I like the ones up here now – they're all right but I don't think I'd like any other ones I've not yet met',

'I thought I'd never get on with Catholics the way I get on now. If you get to know a Catholic pretty well you'd say to yourself, he's not a Catholic he's a Protestant.'

'I think that when you come here you lose that Belfast aggression. Prejudice starts in Belfast 'cos these's a lot of tension and fear in Belfast. This is only twenty people out of one and a half million – you can't bring them all here.'

'We'll still stay in our own areas when we get back to Belfast.'

(*Scene* programme for schools, BBC 1980)

FOR DISCUSSION

▶ In groups of three or four, discuss the Belfast youths' comments.

KEY IDEAS

'Corrymeela is a *symbol* that Catholics and Protestants can work together in real Christian fellowship.

It is a *channel* through which all sorts of people can work together, using all their unique talents to build a new society.

It is a *challenge* not to surrender to apathy or despair but to work courageously for peace and understanding wherever we are.'

(*Corrymeela* leaflet)

FOR YOUR FOLDERS

▶ Write an article of about 150 words on 'The work and aims of Corrymeela'.

▶ *'Your prejudice will harden when you return to Belfast.'* What is prejudice? What sorts of prejudice do these young people have to cope with?

▶ Do you think the aims of Corrymeela can be realized in the troubles of Northern Ireland?

▶ Why is it not easy being a priest in Belfast today?

Our anger is justified . . .

It is, he confesses, not easy being a priest in Belfast today. Clonard Monastery is right in the heart of the Lower Falls area, 50 yards or so from the green barricades that mark the border with the Protestant Shankhill district. He gazes out of a window over the neat Protestant estate just over the wall: "I used to be afraid to go there until quite recently."

He points to a picture of a young monk, Brother Michael Morgan, on the wall opposite the window. "He was shot here as he looked through this window on July 22, 1920. Shot by a British soldier. They thought the monastery was an arsenal for Republicans. They couldn't make the distinction. When the steam gets up every Catholic is a Provo. You can see the parallels."

He is still profoundly shocked by the savagery on view last week: his colleague, Father Alec Reid, was the priest who attempted the kiss of life on one of the soldiers murdered at Saturday's funeral. At times he finds speech difficult and lowers his head into his hands.

A year ago he and Father Reid attempted to negotiate a ceasefire between the two factions of the Irish National Liberation Army indulging in a mutual bloodbath.

He has little sympathy for the argument that Catholic priests should not involve themselves in the funerals of known terrorists. "We will pray for a dead republican, but that's true Catholicity. We will pray for a dead republican, but that's true Catholicity. We will pray for everybody. We'll leave the judgment to God. I will go on trying to be a priest to everybody, to be a witness to the fact that there are no

outsiders in God's heart. It doesn't mean you accept them for Communion. Gerry Adams comes for Mass here from time to time." He pauses. "We don't say to him 'You can't come' . . ." His voice trails off.

He recites his own poem calling on freedom fighters to end their war and accept "the violence of God's love." He hesitates before the last verse because "it seems to be almost aligning yourself with the butchery." It runs:
Go home to your children,
*   British soldier*
Go home to your wife with
*   your pay*
Go home . . .
With our Father's love upon you
And we'll surely find His way

He lowers his head again. "It's so hard to say the right thing." Involved as he is with the families of those in prison for the Birmingham bombings, he has found it particularly hard to maintain the levels of forgiveness he knows he should. "I know I must forgive. I know it is for me to reach out to Lord Denning. He is imprisoned in his own cultural back-ground. I know I must reach out to the people who beat the Birmingham Six black and blue for those who really planted the Birmingham bombs. In my heart I know I am so far from that, but that's the only kind of love that will transform the situation."

Father Reynolds believes the mainland churches now have a crucial role to play: "If I say things it sounds as if I'm talking out of cultural prejudice. More and more I'm coming to be convinced that it is for the church in Britain to help the British people to understand and to forgive."

(*The Guardian*, 26 March 1989)

32 L'ARCHE COMMUNITY

Jean Vanier has been called a 'modern day saint of the poor and servant of the handicapped'. In this reflection he talks about his life:

REFLECTION

'In 1963 I was teaching philosophy at the university of Toronto. While in France I went to visit a priest who was chaplain for 30 men with a mental handicap. It was the first time in my life (I was 35) that I met people who had a mental handicap. I was amazed and bewildered and somehow a little bit overwhelmed. The cry of anger in those men, and sometimes even violence, their deep sadness, and at the same time their incredible cry for relationship.

These men seemed so different from my students at the university who were more or less interested in my head and in what they could get out of it in order to pass their exams, but they were not at all concerned with my person. These men I met could not care less about what was in my head and about philosophy; they were interested in my person. They craved friendship, relationship, where they would be seen as unique. Somehow their cry evoked something deep in me. But at the same time I was overwhelmed by their needs.

This is how I became interested in the plight of these people and I began visiting asylums and hospitals. In them I saw many men and women living in crowded and most unbearable conditions.

And so it was that a few months later, I bought a house and I invited two men to come and live with me. Both had metal handicaps. Neither had any family as their parents had died. They had been put into a dismal institution.

We started living together in a small rather dilapidated house. We began to discover each other. They had their anger and fears but also their hopes. Little by little I discovered the immense pain hidden inside the loneliness they felt, their broken self-image, because they had been pushed around so much in life and had received so little respect. I also came to know their incredible goodness.

Other people came to help and so we were able to welcome more handicapped people. My idea was to create a little "home", or family. I did not want L'Arche (the name given to that first home) to be an institution but a community where each person had his or her place, where we could work, grow, celebrate and pray together.

The French government recognized us, it was in need of places to welcome people with mental handicaps. We were able to buy another home in the village and little by little we grew. There are now some 400 people in our community, in many small homes scattered in villages. Each home is as independent as possible.

Other people from other countries came to visit or to live with us for a while. Some were deeply touched by their experience here and began to found similar communities in their own country. And now there are over 90 communities in 20 different countries. In England there are four communities in London, Liverpool, Bognor Regis and near Canterbury. There are communities in Inverness in Scotland, Kilkenny in Ireland, in Calcutta, in Honduras, in Burkina Faso in Africa. Each one is inspired by the same spirit and lives off the same principle: to create community.

The inspiration at the basis of each community is religious, but the ways of expressing the love of God may be different. I myself am Roman Catholic, and the first community of L'Arche was inspired by my faith. We wanted the community to be a place of love and hope, a place of sharing, a place where people could find peace of heart and forgiveness. We wanted L'Arche to be a place where the poorer person was at the centre and not the "helpers". In England our communities welcome predominantly Christians from the Anglican tradition. Very quickly our homes there became ecumenical. In India our communities are essentially made up of Hindus, Muslims and Christians. Yes, our differences are sometimes painful, but we are learning that the poor can call us to unity.

Many things happen in our communities. There are crises of all sorts. Some people need good psychological help; some take a long time to find any peace of heart or healing. Some like to work; others hate it. There is joy, there is pain; it is the joy and the pain of living together.

Most of the people we welcome are called to be with us all their lives. A few leave and get married. But the majority are much too severely wounded. Assistants come for periods of one or two years, and more and more are putting their roots down in the community, making a life commitment into the family. This is essential. There are so many people *in institutions who are yearning for a network of friendship and community. But there are few people in society willing to climb down the ladder of success and to become a brother or sister to a person with a mental handicap.*

Our society sees the world in the form of a ladder: there is top and bottom. We are encouraged to climb that ladder, to seek success, promotion, wealth and power. At L'Arche, in living with our wounded brothers and sisters, we are discovering that to live humanly, it is not that ladder that we should take as a model, but rather to see the world as a body. In a body there are many different parts, each one is important, even the smallest and the weakest.

People with a mental handicap who come to our communities are called to rise up in hope and to discover the beauty of their beings. Those who come to help are called to see what is most beautiful in their own hearts. And thus the body is formed. We discover we are linked together.

And because we are linked together, we learn to forgive each other for we can so easily hurt one another when we live together. We learn to celebrate the fact that we have been called together. Little by little, we become people of joy because we are people of prayer, people of covenant relationship.'

(Jean Vanier, Resurgence 110, May/June)

For further information on L'Arche and Jean Vanier, the following books are suggested:
Community and Growth, Jean Vanier, Darton, Longman & Todd, 1979
The Broken Body, Jean Vanier, Darton, Longman & Todd, 1988

FOR YOUR FOLDERS

▶ How did Jean Vanier become interested in the plight of mentally handicapped people?
▶ What are the needs of these people?
▶ What is the inspiration behind L'Arche?
▶ What difficulties do you think people encounter in these communities?
▶ *'The world is a body not a ladder.'* Explain carefully after reading this reflection what this means.

Jean Vanier (third from right)

33 WORSHIP – AN INTRODUCTION

REFLECTION

'Often I think of that beautiful old song by Louis Armstrong, "I see friends shaking hands saying How do you do, they're really saying 'I love you', and I think to myself, what a wonderful world." Despite the sufferings of the world I often feel a great sense of wonder about our lives on this beautiful planet and in this enormous and mysterious universe. Every single day is both a miracle and a challenge in itself. The miracle of love, of new life, of friendships, of beauty, of the power and complexity of nature. The challenges of being human and trying to live an honest, caring life. Something inside of me compels me to worship the Cause of all this. I need to say "Thank you" to this Cause, this Energy, which I as a Christian call God. When I worship I struggle to find that deep quiet within. That peace that passeth all understanding, that lies within us, beyond the mad rushings of the mind. When I worship I am making a quiet journey within to meet the Lord and Saviour. I know that He is waiting, ready, to pour out His grace and love to me. I know and feel that when I worship I am alive and I am being human. I know that God has given us freedom to choose and that by acknowledging Him, I am fulfilling myself and being what I am truly supposed to be – a child of God's universe.'

(Ellen Jenkins, author's interview)

For Christians, worship, like all other aspects of belief and practice, is centred around beliefs about Jesus Christ. An important feature of Christian worship is the way that Christians regularly gather together with other believers for public acts of worship. Another feature is the way that Christians will sometimes worship privately, on their own or with their families. Most public acts of worship take place on a Sunday and in a church building. In most Christian denominations, individual members of the congregation take part in the practices of regular worship. Many Christian denominations have a full-time professional staff of clergy (see unit 36) who are in charge of the churches and lead the worship.

Differences of style

LITURGICAL OR FORMAL WORSHIP

'Liturgy' is a Greek word meaning 'public worship'. In this style of worship, the activities are all set out in a **liturgy** (certain pattern). Liturgical worship often tends to be very formal, elaborate and colourful, with many rituals. This type of worship is usually common in Christian churches that have a high regard for the sacraments (see unit 46), for instance the Roman Catholic and Orthodox Churches. In these churches beliefs are expressed through the use of many symbolic objects and actions.

NON-LITURGICAL WORSHIP

In this style of worship, set rituals and symbolic actions are avoided. This worship is common among many Protestant churches. The emphasis is more on practises like Bible readings, prayers, hymns and sermons. Although the sacraments of Baptism and Holy Communion may still be used, the main emphasis is on the spoken and written message of Christianity. An example of a less formal style of worship can be found among the Society of Friends (see unit 24).

These two very different styles of worship reflect different basic emphases. Christians who follow liturgical styles of worship see worship as being 'sacramental'. The word **sacrament** (see unit 46) means 'a religious rite followed as an outward and visible sign of an inward and invisible spiritual grace'. In other words, emphasis is put on many outward signs and symbols which express deep religious and spiritual feeling and meaning.

For Christians who follow less formal styles of worship, the emphasis is on the 'word of God' (see unit 21). Because of this, worship tends to focus on spoken presentations and responses.

Generally, for Christians, acts of worship:

- enable them to express and declare their faith;
- inspire and strengthen them in their daily lives;
- provoke responses like praise, thanksgiving, joy, love, wonder, commitment and repentance;
- can be expressed through art, music, burning of incense, clapping, communion, ringing of bells, prayers, kissing of icons, lighting of candles, reciting creeds, silence, Bible readings, sprinkling of holy water, greeting others, making the sign of the cross, story telling, wearing of special clothes, offering of money.

FOR YOUR FOLDERS

▶ What does worship mean for Ellen Jenkins? How does it enable her to express her faith? What responses does worship provoke in her?

▶ What are the differences between liturgical and non-liturgical styles of worship?

▶ What differences in styles of worship would you expect to find between a Society of Friends and an Orthodox Church service?

'When I worship I struggle to find that deep quiet within'

'True Christian worship includes the love of God and the love of neighbour' (Archbishop Desmond Tutu)

REFLECTION

'We all have the need to worship – to worship something or someone greater than ourselves, to whom we wish to dedicate our whole lives. Sometimes they say we all have a God-shaped space inside us and only God can fill it. This means that we are created by God, we are created like God, and we are created for God. And since God is infinite, you and I are made for the infinite and nothing less than God can really ever satisfy our hunger for God.

Others try to worship things that are less than God – it may be money, or ambition, or drugs or sex. In the end they find out that they are worthless idols. To worship means to give due worth to someone or something. We give worth to God. Worship is absolutely central to our faith where God comes first, always. We bow before His infinite majesty and holiness, trembling with awe at His unapproachable light and radiance. Many times we feel that words are utterly inadequate, so we keep a deep silence in the holy presence. But true Christian worship can never let us be indifferent to the needs of others, to the cries of the hungry, of the naked and the homeless, of the sick and the prisoner, of the oppressed and the disadvantaged.

True Christian worship includes the love of God and the love of neighbour. The two must go together or your Christianity is false. We are Christian not only in church on Sunday. Our Christianity is not something we put on like our Sunday best. It is for every day. We must worship our God for ever and ever, and serve Him by serving our neighbour today and always.'

(Archbishop Desmond Tutu, Hope and Suffering, William Collins 1983)

In general the Christian religion has three important features – doctrine (statements about beliefs), deeds and worship. Although all three are distinct they cannot be separated. To understand what Christians are doing when they worship you need to consider these other features, because Christian worship is linked to what Christians believe and what they do. If we look at Desmond Tutu's reflection on worship we can see that for him true Christian worship includes 'serving our neighbour today and always'.

Christian belief

As we have seen in previous units, Christians believe that this visible and physical world is not the only reality. They believe that above, within and beyond the sights and sounds of this world lies another reality. The word **transcendent** is often used to describe this other reality. 'Transcendent' means 'going beyond ordinary limits'.

The idea of a 'transcendent reality' has been expressed by poets and writers through the ages. In this poem by the Christian writer Francis Thompson, the link between the physical world and the transcendent world is made:

> 'O World Invisible, we view thee,
> O World Intangible, we touch thee,
> O World Unknowable, we know thee,
> Inapprehensible, we clutch thee.'
>
> (Francis Thompson, 'The Kingdom of God', *Penguin Book of Religious Verse*, Penguin 1963)

Christians feel that there are many ways of 'viewing, touching, knowing and clutching' this 'invisible, intangible, unknowable, inapprehensible' reality. Expressions of such things within the Christian religion can take many forms. Just a few examples might include:

- listening to great works of music;
- reading the holy scriptures;
- expressing transcendent ideas in great architecture;
- by prayer, contemplation, silence and deep thought.

Christian deeds

For Christians, what they do in their lives is clearly connected with what they believe about life. Christian belief cannot be separated from worship, so in their lives Christians try to act out of love, as

they believe Jesus Christ did. However, they believe that because they are far from perfect they cannot act without God's help – this help is called **grace**. Worship helps Christians to get close to God, who gives them the grace to face life with all its problems and challenges.

TALKING POINT

- 'True Christian worship can never let us be indifferent to the needs of others, to the cries of the hungry, of the naked and the homeless, of the sick and the prisoner, of the oppressed and the disadvantaged.'
  (Desmond Tutu)

KEY IDEAS

There are generally two important activities in Christian worship:

- offering – this means all that goes out from the worshipper, e.g. praise, adoration, confession;
- receiving – this means all that comes back, e.g. fellowship, forgiveness, inspiration, strength.

FOR YOUR FOLDERS

▶ *'We all have the need to worship'* – explain Desmond Tutu's words.
▶ Explain in detail what Desmond Tutu means by *'True Christian worship'*.
▶ Explain what the word 'transcendent' means. Explain some of the ways that Christians might try to 'touch' the transcendent.
▶ Explain the word 'grace'. How do you think worship helps Christians in their everyday lives?

The ways in which Christians worship can take many forms. In this unit we shall look at two very distinctive styles of Christian worship.

The Eastern Orthodox Church

Two of the main features of worship in the Orthodox Church are the use of icons and the importance that is attached to symbolic actions.

Icons (see unit 23) are religious pictures of Jesus, scenes from the Crucifixion, or saints such as Peter or Mary, the mother of Jesus. Their purpose is to remind worshippers that in worshipping God, they are joining with the saints in heaven. All Orthodox churches have a screen dividing the main part of the church from the inner sanctuary. This screen is called an 'iconostasis', which means 'place of the icons, or pictures'. The iconostasis is usually covered with icons. In the centre of the screen there are doors which are opened at several points during Holy Communion to reveal the **altar**. The iconostasis screen stands for the separation between heaven and earth, and God and people. When the doors are opened it reminds the worshippers that God has ended that separation in the person of Jesus Christ.

The other main feature of worship in the Eastern Orthodox Church is the importance of symbolic actions. During the actual service members of the congregation often move around. A worshipper might feel the need to light a candle and will walk around the church in order to do so. When worshippers arrive at the church they buy a small candle, light it and place it on a stand before an icon.

In Eastern Orthodox churches there are no pews or rows of chairs. The worshippers stand together in groups and they kneel, or bow the knee (called 'genuflecting'), or touch the ground with their foreheads during certain parts of the service. All these movements have symbolic meaning. For instance, by touching the forehead on the ground, worshippers express things like submission to God.

Orthodox churches are ornately and beautifully decorated

Friends sit quietly together at a meeting

The Society Of Friends ('Quakers')

The Society of Friends (also known as 'Quakers') meet for worship in a simple room or building. These rooms, called 'meeting houses', have no special decorations, furniture or symbols. Quakers have no fixed form of service and they do not believe in having any outward images.

The chairs are set in a square with a table in the centre – usually with some copies of the Bible on it, and perhaps some flowers. The Friends sit quietly together in silence. The silence can last for the whole hour of the meeting, or sometimes less. During this time someone will stand and speak for a few minutes and then sit down. What is shared might be a personal testimony, a reading from the Bible, or a poem may be read out. This is sometimes referred to as 'ministry'. At the end of an hour, one of the leaders (called 'elders') will bring the meeting to a close.

For many Friends the focus of the meeting will be their awareness of the living presence of Jesus, through the events of His life or of something that He said which is specially meaningful to them. This is one of the reasons that Quakers have never observed the Eucharist. They believe that to symbolize the presence of Jesus using bread and wine is unnecessary, because in their quiet meetings they believe they are aware of His presence with them.

No hymns are sung, no sermon is spoken, no prayer books are used, and there is no altar, pulpit or organ in Quaker meetings. The meeting begins when the first person arrives, sits down and waits quietly in silence. Others enter the room and share in this stillness.

The quietness of a Quaker meeting provides an ideal setting for members to explore themselves, God and their relationship to other people.

FOR YOUR FOLDERS

► Explain the following words: icons; iconostasis; elders; ministry.
► Look at the photographs. Write a paragraph on each, describing:
  a what you see;
  b the differences between the pictures.
► Write a paragraph about 'The symbolism of Eastern Orthodox worship'.
► What do you think are the most important features of Quaker worship?
► Explain the views held by Quakers and Eastern Orthodox Christians about the Eucharist.

THINGS TO DO

► How do the interiors (see photographs) of these places of worship reflect the different beliefs of the two groups of worshippers?

36 PLACES OF WORSHIP

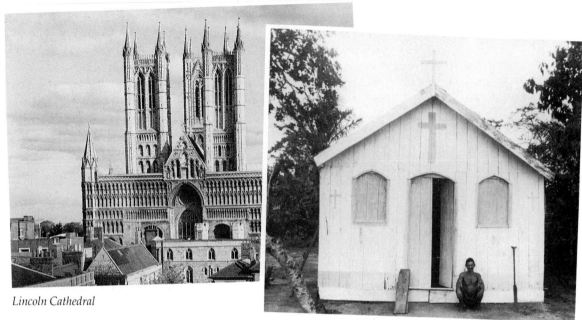

Lincoln Cathedral

A small church in an Amazon clearing

For most local Christian groups the centre of their religious lives revolves around a church building. In this unit we shall look at some of the many differences to be found in Christian places of worship, and the way that these differences reflect different Christian attitudes to belief and practice.

Some Christian groups believe that the building or place of worship is not important at all. For them, too much emphasis on material things like church buildings can be an obstacle to their faith. Others, like Quakers, might have a building which they keep as simple as possible, with few furnishings or decorations. However, many Christian groups see places of worship as being sacred or holy. They believe that these holy places must have their own special character and atmosphere which enable worshippers to sense the presence of God and respond with reverence and devotion.

Here are some characteristics of Christian places of worship. Note how they often reflect the different emphases that different Christian groups have:

- Many places of worship, like cathedrals (from Latin 'cathedra' meaning 'bishop's throne'), are beautifully decorated and furnished to create an atmosphere that helps the worshipper to experience God's splendour and glory.
- The central and most holy part of many churches, like Anglican and Roman Catholic churches, is the 'holy table' or **altar**. Many Christians feel that the altar is the place where Jesus' presence is most deeply felt during the Eucharist.

- In most church services somebody preaches, and the place they preach from is usually high enough for the congregation to see and hear them. This is known as the 'pulpit', usually made of wood or stone and reached by a few steps. In some churches like Methodist churches the pulpit is more prominent than the altar, because Methodists generally place more stress on the presence of God through his word (see figure 1).

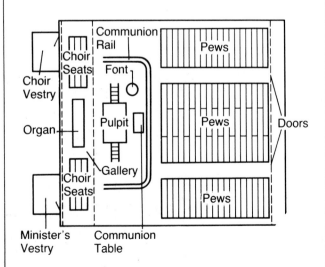

1 Plan of a Methodist church

- Many churches and cathedrals have tall spires pointing to the sky. A spire makes the church easier to see. Others may have a square tower. These remind Christian worshippers to look up to God. Some churches have a bell tower and the bells are rung at special times.
- Many churches and cathedrals have stained glass window decorations, often telling a story or expressing a belief. These windows help to add to the atmosphere of the building.
- Most churches have a carefully thought out structure. Traditional Christian churches have developed the cruciform (in the form of a cross) shape (see figure 2). When the worshippers face the altar they are facing east (where the sun rises), which many Christians feel is symbolic of the resurrection of Jesus.
- In Baptist churches a central feature is the baptistery, or pool. In some Baptist churches the baptistery can be very big. Baptists believe that people should be baptized only when they are old enough to know what they are committing themselves to, so the baptistery occupies a prominent position (see unit 24).
- In other churches a font (a large bowl made of stone that contains the water used for baptism) is often found near the church entrance, because being baptized means entering the church.
- In churches that teach the sacraments there are 'confessionals'. These are wooden constructions that separate the person who is **confessing** his or her sins (the 'penitent') from the priest who is hearing him or her. The person confessing kneels in one part and talks to the priest through a small grille. However, in the Roman Catholic Church it is becoming more usual to remove this barrier, and people confess face-to-face with a priest.
- In the Roman Catholic Church there are small chapels dedicated to the Virgin Mary, containing a statue of her. Also, a light is always kept burning by the altar of Roman Catholic churches, reminding worshippers that God is always present.

FOR YOUR FOLDERS

▶ Explain the following words: pulpit; spire; altar; cruciform; baptistery; font; confessionals; penitent.
▶ Write a sentence about each of the photographs.
▶ How do church buildings reflect some of the beliefs of:
  a Methodists;
  b Baptists;
  c Roman Catholics?
▶ Why are places of worship very important to many Christians?
▶ *'Places of worship are full of symbolism.'* Explain what you think this means.

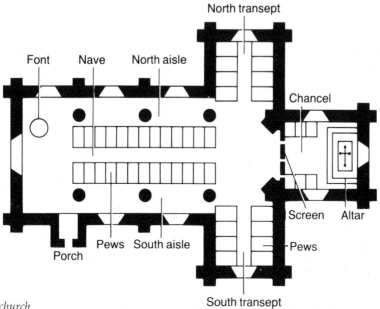

2 Plan of a cruciform church

A Catholic priest celebrates mass

'Then he poured water into a basin and began to wash the disciples' feet' (John 13:5)
In this act of service, Jesus set an example to all Christian leaders. He reminded them that they were there to serve others, and to minister to and help them. This is why some Churches use the word 'minister', when they talk about their religious leaders.

KEY WORD

Ordination – 'the act or ceremony of ordaining a religious leader.'

In the Roman Catholic Church, the Eastern Orthodox Church and the Church of England, the Eucharist (see unit 47) is always carried out by a priest. In some Churches, for example the Methodist Church, it has to be carried out by a fully ordained minister.

Ordination is the ceremony by which a Church appoints its ministers. The most usual ceremony includes the very ancient practice of 'laying on hands'. This is seen as a direct way of passing on spiritual power and authority.

Some Christian denominations feel that ordination is not necessary. However, in some Churches ordination is seen as being extremely important because people feel that the priest or minister is doing work that is so sacred and so important that he needs the authority of the Church to do it.

Before ordination, Roman Catholic, Orthodox and Anglican priests undergo a long period of training. The length of time for this varies, but it can be more than four years before full-time service can begin.

Structures

Churches which have the ministry of bishops are called 'episcopal' (from the Greek word for bishop). They are the Roman Catholic, Orthodox and the Anglican Churches. These churches have three orders of ministry – bishops, priests and deacons. Bishops are in charge of large areas called dioceses. Most priests work in a parish, or local community. In Britain, deacons are people about to become priests.

Archbishops have even more responsibility than bishops. They can sometimes be in charge of the whole Church in one country. In the Orthodox Church the senior archbishops are called 'patriarchs' (which means great fathers). In the Roman Catholic Church an extremely important group called the cardinals is responsible for electing the Pope. In England, Anglican bishops and archbishops are appointed by the Queen who is the Head of the Church of England. Many Protestant churches elect their national leaders (sometimes called moderators) every year, and these people rule their groups through councils which are elected by individual churches.

Women priests

The Roman Catholic and Eastern Orthodox Churches have no women priests. Some Churches that do have women priests include the Lutheran Churches, The French Reformed Church, The Congregationalists, the Methodists and the Baptists. At present there is an enormous debate within the Anglican Church about the ordination of women. This is causing deep division within the Church (see unit 59).

Work

Generally speaking, in Christian worship, the minister has two jobs: he acts as the representative of the community; and he is used as the means by which God addresses the people, by preaching and reading from the scriptures. A minister's work within the community can cover a whole range of activities. These can include things like running

youth groups; visiting prisoners, elderly people and people in hospital; counselling the bereaved, the sick, the lonely and the depressed; helping with fund-raising activities; organizing the running of the parish; and much more. Some ministers are chaplains. They do not have a parish but work in the armed forces, or in prisons, universities or factories instead.

FOR YOUR FOLDERS

► Explain the following words: minister; ordination; episcopal; deacon; cardinal; patriarch; moderator.
► Why do you think Christian leaders are sometimes called 'servants in authority'?
► Construct a diary for a priest or minister. You will have to use your imagination to describe how his or her week is spent.

THINGS TO DO

► Look at this extract from the ordination service in the Anglican Church. Make a list of some of the duties of a priest.

Before the Bishop ordains a Priest, he addresses the candidate with the following words . . .

A priest is called by God to work with the bishop and with his fellow-priests, as servant and shepherd among the people to whom he is sent. He is to proclaim the word of the Lord, to call his hearers to repentance, and in Christ's name to absolve, and to declare the forgiveness of sins. He is to baptize, and prepare the baptized for Confirmation. He is to preside at the celebration of the Holy Communion. He is to lead his people in prayer and worship, to intercede for them, to bless them in the name of the Lord, and to teach and encourage by word and example. He is to minister to the sick, and prepare the dying for their death. He must set the Good Shepherd always before him as the pattern of his calling, caring for the people committed to his charge, and joining with them in a common witness to the world.

Almighty God, give us priests:
to establish the honour
    of your holy name;
to offer the holy sacrifice of the altar;
to give us Jesus
    in the holy sacrament;
to proclaim the faith of Jesus;
to baptize and to teach the young;
to tend your sheep;
to seek the lost;
to give pardon to the penitent sinner;
to bless our homes;
to pray for the afflicted;
to comfort mourners;
to strengthen us in our last hour;
to commend our souls.
Almighty God, give us priests!

Holy father, you gave us Christ as the Shepherd of our souls; may your people always have priests who care for them with his great love.

We make our prayer through Jesus Christ our Lord, who lives and reigns with you and the Holy Spirit, one God, for ever and ever. Amen.
(From the Ordination of Priests in the Alternative Services Book, Church of England 1980)

Different Churches put different emphases on the Christian calendar. For instance, the Roman Catholic Church keeps a very full calendar, observing a great many feasts and saints' days. Some Protestant Churches, on the other hand, keep a much simpler calendar, with only major festivals being observed. Some Evangelical Churches ignore the traditional Christian calendar completely, except for Christmas and Easter.

In the Christian calendar many **festivals**, sometimes called **fasts** and **feasts**, do not fall on the same date each year. The only two feasts that have the same date every year are **Christmas** (25 December) and **Epiphany**, which is related to Christmas. Saints' Days, which celebrate the death of Christian saints, also fall on the same date each year. However, if that date happens to fall on a Sunday (which is always a feast day), then the Saint's Day will be moved to another date.

The reason why all the other festival dates vary is because they depend on the date of **Easter**. The rule for determining the date of Easter is quite complicated: Easter Day is always the first Sunday after the full moon which happens around 21 March. If the full moon is on a Sunday, then Easter Day (which is always a Sunday) is the Sunday afterwards.

In the western Church, a tradition has grown of using different coloured robes for the leaders of worship at each season of the Church year. For instance, purple robes are worn during periods of fasting, for example during **Advent** and **Lent**; white robes are worn for the major festivals of Easter, Christmas, Ascension Day and some Saints' Days.

The Christian calendar falls into two main sections, revolving around the festivals of Christmas, when Christians celebrate the birth of Jesus, and Easter, when they remember His death. The festivals are observed by Christians all over the world on the same days. In the two photographs opposite, children in Panama re-enact the birth of Jesus, and children in Guyana act out the events of Good Friday when Jesus was crucified.

The Christian Year

Month	Festival or season
Late November or early December	**Advent** There are four Sundays in Advent leading up to Christmas.
25 December	**Christmas Day**
6 January	**Epiphany** There can be up to six Sundays in Epiphany. If Easter is early there must be fewer.
February/March	**Septuagesima** (70 days before Easter)
February/March	**Ash Wednesday** (The first day of Lent) There are 40 days in Lent, plus six Sundays.
March/April	**Easter Day** There are five Sundays during the season of Easter.
April/May/June	**Ascension Day** Always on the Thursday 40 days after Easter.
May/June	**Pentecost** Sometimes called Whitsun. Always seven weeks after Easter.
May/June	**Trinity Sunday** Always eight weeks after Easter. There can be up to 27 days in the Trinity season.

Children in Panama act out the birth of Christ

Children in Guyana act out the Crucifixion

THINGS TO DO

▶ Look at the photographs. Explain in your own words what Christian festivals these children are celebrating. Write a couple of sentences about each of the photographs.

FOR YOUR FOLDERS

▶ Explain how the date for Easter Day is worked out.
▶ Why do you think that the Christian calendar is important for Christians?

39 CHRISTMAS

Before reading this unit, read the birth stories of Jesus in Matthew's Gospel, chapters 1 and 2.

Christmas is the second most important festival of the Christian year, after Easter. It begins four Sundays before Christmas Day, with the season of Advent.

Advent

The period known as Advent provides an opportunity for Christians to retell and reflect upon many of the Biblical stories and passages which they believe point to Jesus as God's promised Saviour for the human race. For Christians, most of this preparation and reflection takes place during church services when the congregation hears readings from the Scriptures. Some Christian families have an Advent calendar and Advent candles at home which they use in the days leading up to Christmas Day (25 December).

Christmas

The word 'Christmas' comes from the old English 'Chrestes Maesoes', which means 'Christ's Mass'. Nobody really knows the exact date of Jesus' birth; it was not considered important by the early Christians who were more concerned with who Jesus was and what he did.

On Christmas Day itself, the great majority of Christians take part in an act of congregational worship. The style of worship varies in different Christian churches. However, the focus of all the different rituals is the birth of Jesus and the proclamation of beliefs in Him, as the Son of God and Saviour of the world.

For some Christians, the most important event of Christmas is the Eucharist, or **Communion** service. It bears the marks of a celebration – with music, the Eucharistic meal and a procession dominating the service. The first Eucharist of Christmas will probably start at about 11.30 p.m., the night before Christmas Day (called Christmas Eve). This service is often called the Midnight Mass, and it is one of the most popular services in the Christian calendar. The next Eucharist will be on Christmas morning, and Christians try to attend this. In the Eucharist, Christians believe that they 'receive' Christ in the bread and wine, and so the idea of God giving himself to human beings at Christmas is echoed in the service.

Christians believe that at Christmas, they are thanking God for giving the world His only Son who was born as a human being. This idea is known as the **Incarnation** (see unit 3). At many Christmas services the first words of John's Gospel are read out, highlighting the idea that the **Word** (Jesus Christ), although He came from God, is God.

'When all things began, the Word already was. The Word dealt with God, and what God was, the Word was. The Word, then, was with God at the beginning, and through Him all things came to be; no single thing was created without Him. All that came to be was alive with His life, and that life was the light of men.'

(John 1:1–4)

Greek Orthodox Christians celebrate on Christmas Day in Jerusalem

A Christmas sermon on peace

Peace on earth . . .

'This Christmas finds us a rather bewildered human race. We have neither peace within nor peace without. Everywhere paralysing fears harrow people by day and haunt them by night. Our world is sick with war. Yet, the Christmas hope for peace and goodwill toward all men can no longer be dismissed as a kind of pious dream. If we don't have goodwill toward men in this world, we will destroy ourselves by the misuse of our own instruments and our own power. Wisdom born of experience should tell us that war is obsolete. The very destructive power of modern weapons of warfare eliminates even the possibility that war may any longer serve as a solution. And so, if we assume that life is worth living, if we assume that we as a species have a right to survive, then we must find an alternative to war. Let us think anew on the meaning of that Christmas hope: "Peace on Earth, Good Will toward Men." As we explore these conditions, I would like to suggest that modern man really go all out to study the meaning of non-violence, its philosophy and strategy.

If we are to have peace on earth our loyalties must become ecumenical rather than sectional. Our loyalties must transcend our race, our tribe, our class and our nation. We must develop a world perspective. No individual can live alone; no nation can live alone and as long as we try, the more we are going to have war in the world. Now the judgement of God is upon us, and we must either learn to live together as brothers or we are all gong to perish together as fools.

Yet as nations and individuals we are independent. All life is inter-related. We are all caught up in the inescapable network of mutuality, tied into a single garment of destiny. Whatever affects one directly, affects another. We are made to live together because of the inter-related structure of reality. Did you ever stop to think that you can't leave for your job in the morning without being dependent on most of the world? We aren't going to have peace on earth until we recognize this basic fact – that all reality is inter-related.

It's one of the strangest things that all the great military geniuses of the world have talked about peace. The conquerers of old who came killing in the name of peace; Alexander, Julius Caesar, Napoleon were akin in seeking a peaceful world order. Hitler even wrote that everything he did in Germany was for peace. And the leaders of the world today talk eloquently about peace. What's the problem? They are talking about peace as a distant goal, as an end we seek, but one day we must come to see that peace is not merely a distant goal we seek, but it is the means by which we arrive at that goal. We must pursue peaceful ends through peaceful means.

If we are to have peace on earth and goodwill toward men we must realize that all life is sacred. Everyone is someone because everyone is a child of God, made in his image and therefore must be respected as such. Until people see this everywhere, until nations see this everywhere, we will be fighting wars.

If there is to be peace on earth and goodwill toward men, we must believe in the ultimate morality of the universe. Something must remind us once again as we stand in the Christmas seas – on that the universe hinges on moral foundations. We must realize this at Easter too, for Christmas and Easter somehow go together. Christ came to show us the way. Men love darkness rather than light; and they crucified Him, and there on Good Friday, there on the cross it was still dark. But then Easter came, and Easter is an eternal reminder that truth-crushed earth will rise again. Easter justifies the saying, "No lie can live forever". And so this is our faith, as we continue to hope for peace on earth and goodwill toward men: let us know that in the process we have cosmic companionship.'

I have a dream

'I have a dream that one day men will rise up and come to see that they are made to live together. I still have a dream that people will be judged on the basis of the content of their character rather than the colour of their skin, and every man and woman will respect the dignity and worth of human personality. I still have a dream today that one day justice will roll down like water, and righteousness like a mighty stream. I still have a dream today that one day war will come to an end, that men will beat their swords into ploughshares and their spears into pruning hooks, that nations will no longer rise up against nations, neither will they study war any more. I still have a dream that one day the lion will lie down with the lamb and every man will sit under his trees and none shall be afraid. I still have a dream today that one day every valley shall be exalted and every mountain and hill be made low, the rough places made smooth and the crooked places straight, and the glory of the Lord shall be revealed and all flesh shall see it together. I still have a dream that with this faith we will be able to adjourn the councils of despair and bring new light into the dark chambers of pessimism. With this faith we will be able to speed up the day when there will be peace on earth and goodwill toward men. It will be a glorious day, the morning stars will sing together and the sons and daughters of God will shout for joy.'

(Martin Luther King, The Trumpet of Conscience, Hodder & Stoughton 1968)

FOR YOUR FOLDERS

▶ Explain the following words and phrases: Advent; Christmas; Incarnation; the Word.

▶ Why do you think Christmas is such an important festival?

▶ What is Dr Martin Luther King's Christmas message to the world?

TALKING POINT

● 'All life is inter-related. Whatever affects one directly, affects another. We are made to live together because of the inter-related structure of reality.'

40 THE MEANING OF CHRISTMAS

In this reflection, the Reverend Richard Roberts, a minister of the Church of Wales, explains what Christmas means for him:

REFLECTION

'Forget the tinsel and the gaudy lights; forget the carol singing and the carousing parties; forget the shops and trees laden with presents – all very enjoyable in the middle of winter, but mostly irrelevant and in no way useful to discover the meaning of the great Christian festival.

We forget, or at least tend to forget, that when "Jesus was born in Bethlehem of Judea in the days of Herod the king", as the Gospel story tells us, it was not like that at all. The hotel where the holy Family had hoped to shelter was full and so the Christ child, the "Light of the World", first saw the light of day in an outhouse among the litter and the hay.

In a world of dire poverty and cruel injustice, a world of greed and selfishness, a child is born, not in some expensive cot in a private nursery but in a mean manger, "where oxen feed on hay". A thing to scandalize the conventional comfortable well-off people of every nation in every age – and yet for Christians the world over, the birth of Jesus signifies the coming of God into our world; of God taking our human nature to reveal to us his Divine Nature – and at His coming, He found His first home to be a very make-shift affair.

The Christmas message is really about involvement. People with ideas who want to change things and influence others, people who feel passionately about something important, have to be involved and Christians believe that when Jesus was born God himself became involved in the life of humanity, in order to change the existing order of things for the better.

For centuries the Jewish people looked forward to a time when poverty, injustice, war, cruelty would give way to a reign of peace and righteousness, when the "lion would lie down with the lamb".

For Christians, this change was inaugurated by the birth of Jesus and that is the event we joyfully commemorate at Christmas. God himself was involved, to give the whole of His creation a better deal and a purpose to living. Of course many Jewish people found it difficult to accept this and today many people find it difficult to accept the stark reality of this event, and prefer to hide behind the tawdry sentimentality of the occasion.

God became involved. He took the form of a slave, a servant, meeting people as they were and where they were. How unbecoming. How undignified. What sordid behaviour in the sight of those so concerned about their status, their wealth, their power, and who always hide behind the conventional.

But every year, Christmas throws down the challenge to all that is false and evil in the world and calls people to decide what is really important in the process of living.

Our indifference to the needs of those who are suffering hunger or poverty, injustice or sickness is a symbol of our rejection of God. Times don't seem to have changed for it was written down 2000 years ago that, "he entered his own realm, and his own would not receive him" (John 1:11).

Christ's birth tends to upset people's comfortable little lives, and they don't want this to happen. So, they try to keep him out in that outhouse where he was born. So they hide the true message in heaps of pretty tinsel and flashing neon lights.

But those who truly believe in him will try to follow his example. They know that he speaks to them of God in action and in their involvement they will try to change the order of things and make the world a better place to live in. Especially for those who are sick in body and mind, those who are downtrodden, beaten, exploited and hungry in body or in mind.'

(Reverend Richard Roberts, author's interview)

Christian Aid
Christmas Appeal
CHURCHES IN ACTION WITH THE WORLD'S POOR.

Let there be right

The diseases of poverty, like polio and TB, are still crippling millions of children.

Christian Aid is funding work in many parts of the world to change living conditions and give children their right to life.

As Christian Aid's Director, Michael Taylor, says: "What is right is as clear as a bright star in the night sky."

This Christmas it is only right for all of us to join in making a just world for children.

It is time to right wrongs.

JOIN WITH THE POOR TO
MAKE A JUST WORLD
FOR CHILDREN

To: Christian Aid, P.O. Box 100,
London SE1 7RT.

FOR YOUR FOLDERS

▶ Why do people have to 'forget the tinsel and the gaudy lights' to discover the meaning of Christmas, according to Reverend Roberts?

▶ Why does he believe that Christmas is about involvement?

▶ How does Christmas 'throw down a challenge' to people?

▶ How does Christ's birth 'upset people's comfortable little lives'?

THINGS TO DO

▶ Look at the Christian Aid Christmas Appeal. Using some of the ideas you have looked at about Christmas, imagine that Christian Aid or some other charity has asked you to devise a Christmas Appeal.

Pancake Day in Britain

The festival of **Easter** is the most important festival in the Christian calendar, celebrating the death and resurrection of Jesus. It is so important that, for instance, Orthodox Christians often call it 'the feast of feasts'.

Many people think that Easter is a festival that lasts only a few days, from Good Friday to Easter Monday. In fact, the festival lasts for ninety days in all. This period includes the forty days of **Lent** (not including the Sundays) before Easter, and fifty days after Easter (including the Ascension and Whitsuntide).

The period called Lent is associated with the time Jesus spent alone in the wilderness, as recorded in Matthew's Gospel (4:1–17) and Luke's Gospel (4:1–13).

In the early Church, Lent was observed by eating only one small meal in the evening; all animal and fish products were forbidden. Today the observance of Lent is more relaxed and people can choose what to eat. However, some Christians still go on a strict **fast** (they give up eating) for part of the time. Other Christians might observe Lent by giving something up, e.g. sweets, cakes, etc.

The meaning and purpose of Lent, however, has remained the same. It is a time when Christians are reminded that Jesus sacrificed his life for the salvation of all people. Lent is a time when Christians remember too the suffering Jesus endured, in stark contrast to the joy of Easter when Christians remember Jesus' resurrection from the dead.

Shrove Tuesday

The last day before Lent is called Shrove Tuesday. 'Shrove' means 'being forgiven'. It is a time when Christians **confess** their sins and ask God for forgiveness. They often go to a priest who gives them 'absolution' (forgiveness of sins). By doing this they feel that they can have a completely new start for the period of Lent, and can prepare for Easter without feeling burdened by their sins. In Britain, Shrove Tuesday is often called 'Pancake Day', when people eat pancakes, which are made out of flour and eggs. Traditionally, people feasted to eat up all the good things that they might have in their kitchens, before beginning the serious fasting associated with Lent.

Ash Wednesday

The first day of Lent is called Ash Wednesday. In the past, notorious sinners would perform public penance and punish themselves in public to show that they had done wrong and were sorry. Traditionally, small crosses, made from palm leaves which had been used at the previous year's Palm Sunday service, were burnt and the ashes put on people's foreheads in the shape of a cross.

Sundays

Lent is broken up by the weekly festivals of Sundays. The fourth Sunday in Lent is called 'Refreshment Sunday'. It is also known as 'Mothering Sunday', when people show their gratitude to their mothers for their love and care. The fifth Sunday is called 'Passion Sunday' and is a time when Christians think about the final week in Jesus' life (often called 'Holy Week'). Around this time Lent becomes a very solemn and sad time. Some churches cover up all icons, ornaments, crosses, etc. with purple cloths, to introduce feelings of sorrow, sadness and mourning to Lent. This is because during Holy Week, Christians believe that God's only Son was brutally and violently killed on the cross by an ignorant humanity. For Christians it is the darkest time in human history.

The temptation of Jesus

'Full of the Holy Spirit, Jesus returned from the Jordan, and for forty days was led by the Spirit up and down the wilderness and tempted by the devil.

All that time he had nothing to eat, and at the end of it he was famished. The devil said to him, 'If you are the Son of God, tell this stone to become bread.' Jesus answered, 'Scripture says, "Man cannot live on bread alone."'

Next the devil led him up and showed him in a flash all the kingdoms of the world. 'All this dominion will I give to you,' he said, 'and the glory that goes with it; for it has been put in my hands and I can give it to anyone I choose. You have only to do homage to me and it shall be yours.' Jesus answered him, 'Scripture says, "You shall do homage to the Lord your God and worship him alone."'

The devil took him to Jerusalem and set him on the parapet of the temple. 'If you are the Son of God,' he said, 'throw yourself down; for Scripture says, "He will give his angels orders to take care of you", and again, "They will support you in their arms for fear you should strike your foot against a stone."' Jesus answered him, 'It has been said, "You are not to put the Lord your God to the test."'

So, having come to the end of all his temptations, the devil departed, biding his time.'

(Luke 4:1–13)

FOR YOUR FOLDERS

► Explain what happens on Shrove Tuesday and Ash Wednesday.
► Why do Christians see Lent as being a preparation for Easter?
► How might Lent be observed by some Christians?
► What is the meaning of Lent for Christians?
► How might the account of the temptation of Jesus be related to Lent?
► Explain why Lent is often seen as being a time of remembrance and reflection for Christians.

Holy Week, the last week of Jesus' life, is the most solemn time in the Christian year. Holy Week is often called 'The Passion'.

Sunday – Palm Sunday

On this day Christians remember the entry of Jesus into the city of Jerusalem, as recorded in the Gospels.

> 'and those who went ahead and the others who came behind shouted, "Hosanna! Blessings on him who comes in the name of the Lord!'
>
> (Mark 11:9)

On Palm Sunday worshippers are given a small cross made out of palm leaf. In the Gospel accounts it is recorded that people welcomed Jesus by carpeting his path with palm leaves as he rode into the city. Then the worshippers, led by somebody carrying a cross, make a small procession around the church. This is the last celebration for Christians before they enter the sadness of the rest of Holy Week.

Thursday – Maundy Thursday

The word 'Maundy' comes from the Latin word 'mandatum', which means commandment. On Maundy Thursday Christians remember Jesus' last supper with his disciples before his arrest and trial. In the Gospels it is recorded that Jesus shared the meal with his disciples and used the bread and wine as mysterious symbols of his own body and blood:

> 'During supper he took bread, and having said the blessing he broke it and gave it to them, with the words: "Take this; this is my body." Then he took a cup, and having offered thanks to God he gave it to them; and they all drank from it. And he said, "This is my blood, the blood of the covenant, shed for many."'
>
> (Mark 14:22–25)

This meal has become known by different names, e.g. the **Eucharist**, **Mass**, **Holy Communion**. It is regarded by Christians as being the most holy act of worship in the Church (see unit 47). In John's Gospel, it is recorded that Jesus gave his disciples a new commandment at the Last Supper:

> 'I give you a new commandment: love one another; as I have loved you, so you are to love one another. If there is this love among you, then all will know that you are my disciples.'
>
> (John 13:34–35)

On Palm Sunday worshippers are given a small cross made out of a palm leaf

Friday – Good Friday

In the Gospels it is recorded that after the Last Supper Jesus was arrested and put on trial. On the Friday he was crucified by the Romans. The Friday of Holy Week is called 'good' because Christians believe that on that day Jesus displayed the greatest possible sort of goodness, by sacrificing himself on the cross for the sake of humanity.

> *'They brought him to the place called Golgotha, which means "Place of a skull". He was offered drugged wine, but he would not take it. Then they fastened him to the cross. They divided his clothes among them, casting lots to decide what each should have.*
>
> *The hour of the crucifixion was nine in the morning, and the inscription giving the charge against him read, "The king of the Jews." Two bandits were crucified with him, one on his right and the other on his left.'*
>
> (Mark 15:22–28)

This is the most solemn day of the whole Christian year, a day of great sadness and deep emotion. Church services might take place from noon until three in the afternoon. On Good Friday the churches are dark and sombre, reflecting the mood of Christians who believe that the death of Jesus marked the ultimate 'turning away from God'.

The Crucifixion by Salvador Dali

FOR YOUR FOLDERS

▶ Explain in detail:
  a the events of Holy Week as recorded in Mark's Gospel;
  b the ways that Christians remember Holy Week in their beliefs and practices.

THINGS TO DO

▶ Look carefully at the picture of the Crucifixion. Write a review of the picture trying to explain what you think the artist is trying to express.

Sunday – Easter Sunday

It is recorded in the Gospels that three days after his death on the cross, Jesus 'rose from the dead'; this is known as the Resurrection.

> 'When the Sabbath was over, Mary of Magdala, Mary the mother of James, and Salome bought aromatic oils intending to go and anoint him; and very early on the Sunday morning, just after sunrise, they came to the tomb. They were wondering among themselves who would roll away the stone from the entrance to the tomb for them, when they looked up and saw that the stone, huge as it was, had been rolled back already. They went into the tomb, where they saw a youth sitting on the right-hand side, wearing a white robe; and they were dumbfounded. But he said to them, "Fear nothing; you are looking for Jesus of Nazareth, who was crucified. He has been raised again; he is not here; look, there is the place where they laid him." '
>
> (Mark 16:1–6)

The Resurrection by Grünewald

THINGS TO DO

▶ Look up the other Gospel accounts of the Resurrection. Make notes and list the differences and similarities between the four accounts. The other accounts can be found in Matthew 28, Luke 24 and John 20.

The Resurrection of Jesus is regarded by nearly all Christians as being the single most important event in the New Testament. Although scholars and theologians have often debated the facts and meanings of the Resurrection, especially over the last century, for Christians it is a wonderful and miraculous act of God.

The significance of the Resurrection is, for many Christians, explained by the words of St Paul:

> 'But the truth is, Christ was raised to life – the firstfruits of the harvest of the dead. For since it was a man who brought death into the world, a man also brought resurrection of the dead. As in Adam all men die, so in Christ all will be brought to life; but each in his own proper place: Christ the firstfruits, and afterwards, at his coming, those who belong to Christ.'
>
> (1 Corinthians 15:20–24)

Worship

In churches all over the world, the atmosphere changes from one of deep sadness for the Crucifixion, to one of deep joy and thanksgiving at the Resurrection. Ornaments are brought back into the churches, silver and gold colours appear and spring flowers decorate every corner. On Easter Eve, many Christians stay awake (keep a 'vigil'). In Roman Catholic churches, large Easter candles (called 'Paschal candles') are lit and carried in. Everyone in the congregation lights his or her own candle from the Paschal candle and the church is flooded with light. The Easter Proclamation is sung, 'Rejoice. Christ has conquered.' The church bells are rung for the first time in three days and Mass is celebrated. Easter Sunday is the most important day in the Christian year. It celebrates the victory of Jesus' resurrection – the victory of life over death, of light over darkness. For Christians, it is the central point of history – the time when death was conquered and God gave the world his only Son, who atoned for the sins of the world.

THINKING POINT

- 'The image of the "man of dust" has been changed into the "image of the man of heaven", by the appearance among us of the resurrected Christ. As a consequence we are all involved with each other, so that whether we speak of man (Adam) or Jesus Christ, each of us must suffer for the other's sake and share in the other's destiny.'

  (Niebuhr Reinhold, The Nature and Destiny of Man, Nisbet 1941–3)

FOR YOUR FOLDERS

▶ Why is the Resurrection so important for Christians?
▶ *'If Christ has not been raised, then our preaching is in vain'* (1 Corinthians 15:14). What do you think St Paul meant by these words?
▶ Explain and describe some of the practices that are associated with the Resurrection in Christian worship.
▶ What do you think are the ideas that Dylan Thomas tried to convey in *'And death shall have no dominion'*?

Many writers and poets through the ages have tried to capture the mood, the meaning and the significance of the Resurrection. In this poem Dylan Thomas tells us that 'death shall have no dominion':

*'And death shall have no dominion.
Dead men naked they shall be one
With the man in the wind and the west moon;
When their bones are picked clean and the clean bones gone,
They shall have stars and elbow at foot;
Though they go mad they shall be sane,
Though they sink through the sea they shall rise again;
Though lovers be lost love shall not;
And death shall have no dominion.*

*And death shall have no dominion.
Under the windings of the sea,
They lying long shall not die windily;
Twisting on rocks when sinews give way,
Strapped to a wheel, yet they shall not break;
Faith in their hands shall snap in two,
And the Unicorn evils run them through;
Split all ends up they shan't crack;
And death shall have no dominion.*

*And death shall have no dominion.
No more may gulls cry at their ears
or waves break loud on the seashores;
Where blew a flower may a flower no more
Lift its head to the blows of the rain;
Through they be made and dead as nails
Heads of the characters hammer through the daisies;
Break in the sun till the sun breaks down,
And death shall have no dominion'.*

(Dylan Thomas, *The Poems*, JM Dent and Sons Ltd 1963)

To these Greek Orthodox Christians in Athens Easter is a powerful experience of the present

As we have seen, **Easter** is the most important festival in the Christian year. To begin to understand the impact it has on Christians throughout the world, read these two accounts of the Easter experience. The first account is from Mario Constantinou, a young Greek who is a member of the Greek Orthodox Church.

REFLECTION

'Lent, when people share in the fast, is a time for reflection and learning about oneself and Christ. Every day with thousands of others we descend upon the small churches in Athens and offer our prayers to God. Then on the Holy Friday, the day when Christ gave us his ultimate sacrifice, the bells toll throughout our land and the body of our Saviour lies shrouded in flowers in all the village churches. In the churches the great Liturgy takes place. Twelve passages are read from the Bible, while we hold lighted candles. The winding sheet, a cloth symbolizing the broken body of our Saviour, is placed in the middle of the church, like a coffin at a funeral. Although this Friday is the darkest day in the history of the world our hymns and chants echo our hopes of the coming glorious Resurrection. On the Saturday we symbolize Christ's burial by carrying the winding sheet around the church three times. We begin to feel the transformation – the casting aside of death and darkness, the coming of life. The priests change their vestments from the colours of despair to the whiteness of joy and life. At midnight the bells throughout the world chime. The priests wait outside before the closed church door – a symbol of the tomb. The doors are opened and the priests come in with candles and lights. The church is a sea of light as we embrace each other, "Christ is risen" echoes through the church and we reply "He is risen indeed". Easter is not just a celebration of the past; it is a powerful experience of the present.'

(Mario Constantinou, author's interview)

This account of the Easter experience is from an Irish Catholic, Caitlin McKenny, who lives in Belfast.

REFLECTION

'On Holy Thursday we celebrate Mass. The priest will wash the feet of some of the congregation – a re-enactment of Christ's humility. Afterwards the altar is stripped of all ornaments. On the Friday, we have a three-hour service of readings and hymns. A reading from Isaiah sums up what this holy day means to me:

"he was led like a lamb to the slaughter . . . without protection, without justice he was taken away; and who gave a thought to his fate, how he was cut off from the world of living men, stricken to the death for my people's transgression."

(Isaiah)

The Saturday is a day of vigil. St Augustine calls it "the mother of all vigils", for all Christian worship springs from this night. Through drama and poetry we act out the central events of our faith. Here we hope and trust that a world of justice and unity will be born from our suffering world. A large candle is marked with alpha and omega, the first and last letters of the Greek alphabet, and is carried into the darkened church. Its light dispels the darkness. Then the Easter proclamation is sung: "Rejoice: Christ has conquered". A service of readings follows, when the whole of history is recalled – from the alpha of the Creation to the omega of the Resurrection. This is a time of great joy and hope; the bells ring; we sing "Glory to God in the highest". People are sometimes baptized, born anew to a life of promise and love. Mass is celebrated, tonight and again tomorrow – the great mystery of Mass floods my soul with a peace that goes beyond any normal understanding. The sacredness of this shared holy meal is the highest form of human activity. We believe that the risen Lord, the risen Christ is with us in the bread we break and the wine we drink.'

(Caitlin McKenny, author's interview)

INTO THE AGE OF SINCERITY

EASTER celebrates the victory of life over death. We rejoice that total love has proved once and for all that hatred, selfishness and sin have no future. They are doomed to end in utter frustration and despair.

That is a religious and moral truth. It is also valid in all human affairs.

At Easter, then, Christians, although conscious of being engaged in a struggle against the power of darkness until the end of time, are already assured of ultimate victory. We can look confidently for the signs that the battle is being won.

Religion has for decades been relentlessly ridiculed and undermined. It stubbornly refuses to die. The hunger for God and absolute values is as urgent today as ever.

Despite the decline in churchgoing nationally there is without question a positive growth of commitment and sincerity. There is among many people, especially the young, an eagerness for prayer and genuine spiritual experience. Faith often means more than it did in the days when the Churches enjoyed social approval and public endorsement.

In social matters we easily overlook what is good and forget the brutality of a bygone age. Worldwide there is now a radical liberation of women from inequality and oppression. We are a more equal and tolerant society. Religious and ethnic minorities, the weak and handicapped are given better protection and opportunities. Compassion is sometimes derided but almost invariably the public responds spontaneously and generously to disasters and world hunger.

On the international scene, nations are becoming aware that the future depends on better stewardship of our planet's limited resources. A sea-change has also transformed international relations. A pragmatic Communist leadership, bowing to economic necessity, now proposes progressive, verifiable disarmament and an opportunity for a new world order. Only rarely are prayers so obviously answered.

(The Universe)

FOR YOUR FOLDERS

▶ After reading Mario's reflection answer the following questions:
   a Explain the 'Liturgy' and 'winding sheet'.
   b What symbolic actions are taking place?
   c Try to express in your own words what the Easter experience means to Mario.

▶ After reading Caitlin's reflection answer the following questions:
   a Explain 'vigil' and 'alpha and omega'.
   b What symbolic actions are taking place?
   c Try to express in your own words what the Easter experience means to Caitlin.

45 ASCENSION DAY, WHITSUN AND TRINITY SUNDAY

The dove is often used as a symbol of the Holy Spirit

Ascension Day

Jesus is taken up to heaven

So, when they were all together, they asked him, 'Lord, is this the time when you are to establish once again the sovereignty of Israel?' He answered, 'It is not for you to know about dates or times, which the Father has set within his own control. But you will receive power when the Holy Spirit comes upon you; and you will bear witness for me in Jerusalem, and all over Judaea and Samaria, and away to the ends of the earth.'

When he had said this, as they watched, he was lifted up, and a cloud removed him from their sight. As he was going, and as they were gazing intently into the sky, all at once there stood beside them two men in white who said, 'Men of Galilee, why stand there looking up into the sky? This Jesus, who has been taken away from you up to heaven, will come in the same way as you have seen him go.'

(Acts 1:6–11)

On the Thursday which falls forty days after Easter Sunday, Christians remember Jesus' Ascension – when he was taken up into heaven. This was the day when his disciples saw him for the last time. In church services Christians remember the Ascension with special prayers and reading from the Scriptures.

Whitsun

According to the Acts of the Apostles, seven weeks after Jesus' Resurrection another important event took place on the day of the Jewish festival of Pentecost, or Shavuot. This was when the power of the Holy Spirit was given to the disciples (see Acts 2:1–4 and unit 4). In the Hebrew Bible there are many references to the way that the Spirit of God inspired the prophets. There is also the promise in Joel 2:28, that this spirit would one day be *'poured out on all flesh'*. Christians believe that the Holy Spirit was given to the disciples and to the whole of humanity on this day.

Pentecost (or 'Whitsun') is seen by Christians as being the birthday of the Christian Church. Traditionally, it is a time of admitting new members to the Church through the rite of **Baptism.** People dress in white, symbolizing pureness and newness, and because of this the day became known as White Sunday, or Whit Sunday or Whitsun.

Trinity Sunday

Trinity Sunday is a time when Christians think about and reflect upon the mystery of the **Trinity**. They are reminded that they do not believe in three Gods but rather only in one (see unit 3). Although they believe in only one God, they remember to think of him in three ways; God the Father, God the Son and God the Holy Spirit.

On Trinity Sunday some Christian denominations ordain people who have completed their training to the ministry. The Church year from Trinity Sunday until Advent is counted in terms of Sundays after Trinity.

All the festivals of Christianity make the claim that there are not three Gods but only one, and so it is appropriate that the last festival of the Church calendar should be devoted to remembering this idea in particular.

FOR YOUR FOLDERS

▶ Explain why you think that it is important that religions have a calendar.
▶ Write an article of about 150 words called 'The important landmarks in the year of the Church'.
▶ Explain in detail how the events of Jesus' life are reflected in the festivals of Christianity.
▶ Festivals are times of *celebration*. Show in detail how the idea of celebration is present in any one Christian festival that you have studied.
▶ Briefly explain the meaning and significance of Ascension Day, Whitsun and Trinity Sunday.

THINGS TO DO

▶ In the last few units you have looked at some of the most important events in the Christian calendar. Try to represent the Christian year in a large drawing or diagram.

To Christians Pentecost is the birth of the Christian Church

46 THE SACRAMENTS

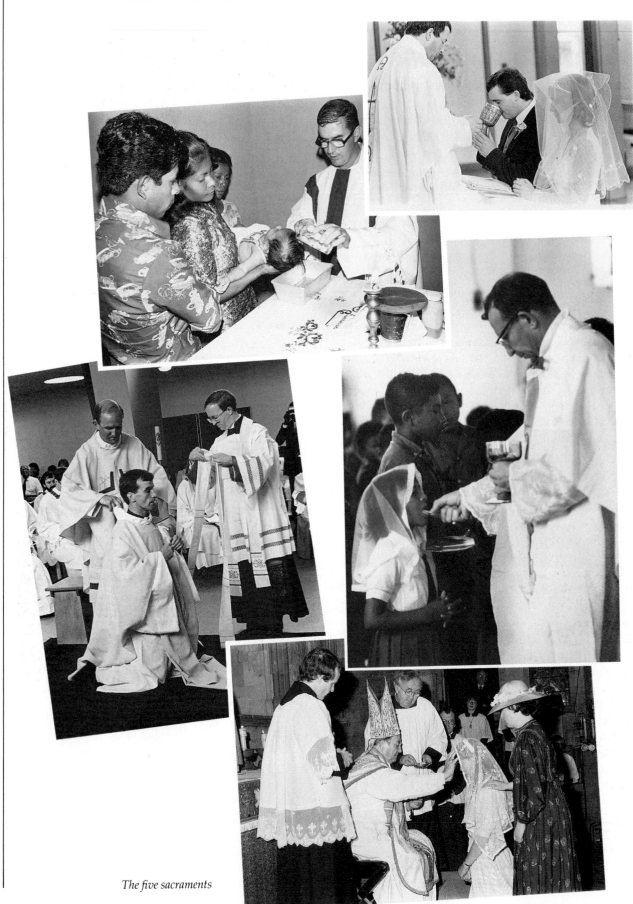

The five sacraments

The Christian scholar St Augustine (354–430 CE) defined a **sacrament** as: *'the visible form of an invisible grace'*.

Quote Nicene Creed handout

All the sacraments involve some physical elements (e.g. bread and wine in the Eucharist). These physical and visible elements represent spiritual and invisible things (e.g. the bread and wine in the Eucharist represent the body and blood of Jesus Christ).

There are a total of seven sacraments:

- The Eucharist;
- Baptism;
- Confirmation;
- Marriage;
- Penance;
- Ordination;
- Anointing of the sick (Holy Unction).

The Roman Catholic and Orthodox Churches accept all the seven sacraments. Christians sometimes call the sacraments 'mysteries'. Most Protestant churches recognize only the first two, the Eucharist and baptism, as being sacraments. Some Christian groups, like the Society of Friends, may not use any sacraments at all.

- **The Eucharist** (see unit 47). This central act of worship re-enacts the death and resurrection of Jesus in ritual form. It remembers the words and actions of Jesus at the Last Supper (see Mark 14:17–25).
- **Baptism** (see unit 49). This is a ceremony in which a child or adult is cleansed of sins, to begin a new life with God.
- **Confirmation** (see unit 49). This is when a baptized person becomes fully accepted into a church. The vows made at his or her baptism are 'confirmed'.
- **Marriage** (see unit 60). This is the sacrament in which a man and a woman promise themselves to each other for life.
- **Penance.** This is sometimes called 'confession'. People confess their sins to a priest, express their sincere sorrow for having sinned, and promise to try not to sin in the future. The priest forgives the sinner in God's name. The effect of penance is to bring the person back to God and the Church. Roman Catholic Christians must confess their sins at least once a year, but the Church encourages people to receive penance more frequently than this.

- **Ordination**. This is the sacrament in which people are made deacons, priests or bishops. Bishops themselves usually take the ordination service and part of this ceremony includes the ancient practice of the 'laying on of hands'.
- **Anointing of the sick.** This is a sacrament given to people who are very sick or very old. The priest anoints the person with oil – a sign of healing. In the Greek Orthodox Church, the anointing of the sick is performed annually in church for the benefit of the whole congregation, on the evening of Holy Wednesday.

FOR YOUR FOLDERS

- ▶ Try to explain in your own words St Augustine's definition of a sacrament.
- ▶ Why do you think the sacraments are sometimes called 'mysteries'?
- ▶ Write a sentence about each of the seven sacraments.
- ! ▶ Why do you think the sacraments are important in Christian faith and practice?

THINGS TO DO

- ▶ Study the five pictures carefully. Explain what you think is happening in each picture and which sacrament is being followed. Remembering St Augustine's definition of a sacrament, try to explain the physical form of each sacrament and what these physical forms represent.

REFLECTIONS

'When we receive Communion, I believe that God reaches out to us on the most primitive and simple level. A babe can receive a small particle of bread and a drop of wine, and with it be reached by God.'
(The Most Reverend Metropolitan Anthony of Sourozh, Head of the Russian Orthodox Church in Britain)

'I cannot do without Mass. If I can see Jesus in the appearance of bread then I will be able to see Him in the broken bodies of the poor. He has said, "I am the Living Bread".'
(Mother Teresa)

'I believe that I receive Christ, not because he is in the bread and wine but because He is in the heart of those who receive the bread and wine believingly.'
(Reverend John Stott, from Gerald Priestland, Pilgrims Progress BBC 1981)

'The bread and wine are distributed to the worshippers on conditions of absolute and complete equality. There is no table of precedence, no priority of duke over dustman, it is an act of total sharing and it is in this act that the Church claims that the life of Christ Himself is shared.'
(S.G. Evans, The Social Hope of the Church, Hodder and Stoughton 1965)

At the centre of the Eucharist is the idea that Jesus died for all human beings

For most Christians the Eucharist is the most important act of worship that takes place in the Christian religion. The word 'Eucharist' comes from a Greek word that means 'thanksgiving'. The Eucharist remembers Jesus' Last Supper as recorded in the Gospels:

'During supper Jesus took bread, and having said the blessing he broke it and gave it to the disciples with the words: "Take this and eat; this is my body." Then he took a cup, and having offered thanks to God he gave it to them with the words: "Drink from it, all of you. For this is my blood, the blood of the covenant, shed for many for the forgiveness of sins."'
(Matthew 26:26–28)

This great act of Christian thanksgiving appears under many different names:

- Breaking of bread;
- Eucharist;
- Lord's Supper;
- Mass (a title often used by Roman Catholic Christians);
- Holy (or Sacred) Liturgy (a title popular among Eastern Orthodox Christians);
- Holy Communion ('Communion' means common sharing).

Christians have sometimes disagreed about what Jesus meant when He said that the bread was His body and the wine His blood. At the centre of the Eucharist for Christians is the idea that Jesus died on the cross for all human beings. By taking part in the meal, Christians feel that they are obeying Jesus' own command to do this in remembrance of Him.

However, there are other interpretations:

- Some Christians see the meal as being a re-enactment of Christ's sacrifice.
- Many Protestant Christians feel that Christ is spiritually present in the Eucharist, as in all acts of worship. The bread and wine are symbols of this presence.
- Others, like Roman Catholic Christians, believe that after the bread and wine have been blessed they somehow mysteriously change. They are no longer just bread and wine, although outwardly their appearance does not change. What happens is that they actually *become* the body and blood of Christ. His body and blood are truly present on the altar. This change is called **transubstantiation**.

Christians who hold this view will not throw away any bread or wine that is left over. Every single crumb of bread and every drop of wine will be consumed. Any complete wafers of bread will be put into a chalice with a lid on it (called a 'ciborium') and kept in a special safe (sometimes called a 'tabernacle') for use another time.

In this extract from his book, *Hymn of the Universe*, Teilhard de Chardin, one of the greatest Christian mystics of this century, explains his ideas about the spiritual significance of bread:

'So, my God, I prostrate myself before your presence in the universe which has now become living flame: beneath the lineaments of all that I shall encounter this day, all that happens to me, all that I achieve, it is you I desire, you I await.

It is a terrifying thing to have been born: I mean, to find oneself, without having willed it, swept irrevocably along on a torrent of fearful energy which seems as though it wished to destroy everything it carries with it.

What I want, my God, is that by a reversal of forces which you alone can bring about, my terror in face of the nameless changes destined to renew my being may be turned into an overflowing joy at being transformed into you.

First of all I shall stretch out my hand unhesitatingly towards the fiery bread which you set before me.. This bread, in which you have planted the seed of all that is to develop in the future, I recognize as containing the source and the secret of that destiny you have chosen for me. To take it is, I know, to surrender myself to forces which will tear me away painfully from myself in order to drive me into danger, into laborious undertakings, into a constant renewal of ideas, into an austere detachment where my affections are concerned. To eat it is to acquire a taste and an affinity for that which in everything is above everything— a taste and an affinity which will henceforth make impossible for me all the joys by which my life has been warmed. Lord Jesus, I am willing to be possessed by you, to be bound to your body and led by its inexpressible power towards those solitary heights which by myself I should never dare to climb. Instinctively, like all mankind, I would rather set up my tent here below on some hill-top of my own choosing. I am afraid, too, like my fellow-men, of the future too heavy with mystery and too wholly new, towards which time is driving me. Then like these men I wonder anxiously where life is leading me . . . May this communion of bread with the Christ clothed in the powers which dilate the world free me from my timidities and my heedlessness! In the whirlpool of conflicts and energies out of which must develop my power to apprehend and experience your holy presence, I throw myself, my God, on your word. The man who is filled with an impassioned love of Jesus hidden in the forces which bring increase to the earth, him the earth will lift up, like a mother, in the immensity of her arms, and will enable him to contemplate the face of God.'

(Teilhard de Chardin, *Hymn of the Universe*, Collins, 1981)

FOR YOUR FOLDERS

- ▶ Explain the main reasons why the Eucharist is regarded by most Christians as being the most important act of worship in the Church.
- ▶ Explain the different interpretations of the Eucharist held by Christians. How might these differences be regarded as being an obstacle to Church unity?
- ! ▶ Explain in your own words the feelings and meanings of the four reflections.

'Christ is in the heart of those who receive the bread and the wine believingly'

In this unit we shall be looking at the way the Eucharist is celebrated and its meaning and significance for Christians.

There are differences in the way the Eucharist is celebrated among the churches but almost all celebrations have a similar pattern:

- **The ministry of the Word** – This is the first part of the service, containing prayers, Bible readings, hymns, acts of confession and perhaps a sermon.

The second major part of the service is the Eucharist proper, and contains the following acts:

- **The taking of the bread and wine** – here worshippers are reminded of the origins of the Eucharist and the bread and wine are put on the **altar** or table;
- **The great thanksgiving (i.e. the Eucharist Prayer)** – Here is an example of the prayer:

It is indeed right,
it is our duty and our joy,
at all times and in all places
to give you thanks and praise,
holy Father, heavenly King,
almighty and eternal God,
through Jesus Christ your only Son our Lord.

For he is your living Word;
through him you have created all things from
the beginning,
and formed us in your own image.

Through him you have freed us from the slavery of sin,
giving him to be born as man and to die upon the cross;
you raised him from the dead
and exalted him to your right hand on high.

Through him you have sent upon us your holy and
life-giving Spirit,
and made us a people for your own possession.

. . . Who in the same night that he was betrayed,
took bread and gave you thanks;
he broke it and gave it to his disciples,
saying,
Take, eat; this is my body which is given for you;
do this in remembrance of me.
In the same way, after supper
he took the cup and gave you thanks;
he gave it to them, saying,
Drink this, all of you;
this is my blood of the new covenant,
which is shed for you and for many for the
forgiveness of sins.
Do this, as often as you drink it,
in remembrance of me.

. . . Therefore, heavenly Father,
we remember this offering of himself
made once for all upon the cross,
and proclaim his mighty resurrection and
glorious ascension.
As we look for his coming in glory,
we celebrate with this bread and this cup
his one perfect sacrifice.
(Alternative Services Book, Church of England 1980)

The breaking of the bread

The bread and wine are blessed or consecrated by the minister or priest. In some churches the words of the Lord's Supper from the Gospels might be read out. Some of the following practices can be associated with this reading:

- bowing or genuflecting (bending of the knee) among the congregation;
- censing (putting incense) around the altar;

- lifting up the bread and the wine;
- ringing the bells.

In some churches members of the congregation might greet each other with the 'sign of peace'. This might involve shaking hands with the people around or embracing them. The sign of peace can represent unity.

The sharing of the bread and wine

In the Orthodox Church Holy Communion is distributed to the congregation by dipping a piece of bread in the wine and then giving it to them on a long spoon.

In Baptist and United Reformed Churches the wine is often distributed in separate glasses by church leaders. People do not drink from the same cup (or 'chalice') but will from their own little cups together.

In the Church of England the congregation receives the bread kneeling at the altar. However, in some Protestant churches the congregation stands round the altar or table in small groups.

The Dismissal

After the receiving of the bread and wine there is a short act of dismissal which might include prayers, a hymn or a blessing. When Roman Catholic Christians attend Mass they follow a sequence which represents a path they believe they must follow in their lives and in their relationship to God. The main steps are as follows:

- they come together as a community in the presence of God (*Fellowship*);
- they turn away from their sin (*Penitential Rite*);
- they listen to the words of God in the Scriptures (*Liturgy of the Word*);
- they give thanks to God (*Eucharistic Prayer*);
- they receive the bread and wine, which they believe has been changed into the body and blood of Jesus Christ (*Communion*), see unit 47;
- they are sent out to serve other people (*Dismissal*).

Other differences

In many Protestant churches a Eucharist may take place once a month. In Roman Catholic churches, Mass takes place daily. In some churches only those people who have been confirmed (see unit 46) are able to take part in the Eucharist, whilst others have no such restrictions.

One important prayer in the Eucharist

The 'Agnus Dei' (Lamb of God), said or sung at the time of the breaking of the bread, has been used in the Christian churches since the end of the seventh century CE:

'Lamb of God, you take away the sins of the world; have mercy on us.
Lamb of God, you take away the sins of the world; have mercy on us.
Lamb of God, you take away the sins of the world; grant us peace.'

This is just one important prayer; there are many others.

FOR YOUR FOLDERS

- ▶ Explain the following words: genuflecting; censing; chalice; consecrated.
- ▶ What does the Eucharistic Prayer tell us of Christian beliefs about:
  a Jesus Christ;
  b the Eucharist?
- ▶ Write an article of about 150 words on the different practices that take place in the Eucharist.
- ▶ In your own words describe how the sequence of the Eucharist for Roman Catholics is applied to their relationship with God.
- ▶ Why do you think that different practices in the Eucharist have emerged in the Christian religion?

The second sacrament accepted by all Christians, except the Salvation Army and the Society of Friends, is **Baptism**. It is the rite of initiation by which people enter the Church. Because of this, in many churches (but not the Baptist Church) the font, which contains the water for baptism, is found near the door of the church.

Baptism is an extremely important part of Christian worship, and it has much meaning and significance.

Baptism is seen by Christians as an act of:

- renunciation ('giving up') – the parents of the baptized child, or the baptized adult, are asked if they repent of their sins and renounce evil;
- renewal – baptism marks the beginning of a new life with God;
- spiritual cleaning – the water used in baptism is a symbol for spiritual and inner cleanliness.

Infant Baptism

Most Christian denominations practise infant baptism. However, some Christians argue that infant baptism is meaningless because the infant is too young to realize and appreciate what is going on. Also, some parents have their children baptized but have no intention of bringing them up in the Christian Church. Here is a reflection by a Baptist:

REFLECTION

'Water is one of life's most important commodities. Small wonder that most religions therefore regard water as a powerful symbol. The early church adopted the practice of baptizing converts in obedience to the instructions Jesus had given to his disciples (Matthew 28:19–20). It was through studying the importance of baptism to the early church that Baptists laid so much stress on the practice which has given them their name.

From time to time Baptists still make use of rivers or seas for baptism. But most Baptist churches nowadays have a baptistery built into the floor of the church. It's a great day when the pool comes into use. The candidate approaches the Minister some weeks before and requests baptism. The minister questions the candidate to make sure he/she has made a personal commitment to Jesus Christ and understands a little of what it means to follow him. Then comes the long-awaited day when the candidate is to confess his or her faith in Jesus Christ. If the candidate is a girl, she will be dressed in a special white baptismal gown. If a boy, he will come dressed in shirt and flannels.

There will be the usual hymns, prayers, readings and sermon. Then, during the hymn before the ceremony, the Minister will leave the church and don his special waders, before returning to the service, and descending the steps leading down to the baptistery. In many churches, the candidate is expected to stand by the pool and to give some sort of statement about how he or she came to faith in Christ. Then once the candidate has entered the water, the Minister pronounces his or her name and plunges the candidate beneath the waters, baptizing him or her "into the name of the Father, the Son and the Holy Spirit". The congregation sings a hymn of faith, while the candidate leaves the baptistery and makes for the dressing room. Quite often the baptismal service is followed by a short celebration of Holy Communion.

What does baptism mean? It is hard to put into words. Baptism, like art or drama, needs to be experienced rather than explained. But clearly the New Testament teaches that baptism is a kind of death and resurrection. It marks the end of an old way of life and the commencement of a totally new quality of life, lived out in the company of all other Christians. Looking at the New Testament baptism is a kind of "statement" – the ceremony speaks very clearly of the way Jesus died and rose again, and how a person needs to be made clean; it is also an act of "commitment" – just as the candidate has taken off his normal clothing and put on his special baptismal attire, so in life he has put the past behind him, and put on a totally new kind of life altogether. Baptism is also a "gift", it is the place where one may receive forgiveness of sins and a means of receiving God's Holy Spirit into life. It is also the gateway into membership of Christ's Church.'

(John Wood, 'The Baptists', Christian Denominations, Pergamon Press 1977)

KEY IDEA

For most Christians, baptism is an outward, visible sign of rebirth. It marks the start of a new life and the water is a symbol of the removal of sin from human life by the death and resurrection of Jesus.

Confirmation

In the early days, when infant baptism became widespread, it became necessary to have a later service which could 'confirm' the undertakings made during baptism. This became known as the rite of **Confirmation**. The promises made on the infant's behalf are made again publicly. The person being confirmed is of an age when he or she will be able to understand these promises. Confirmation services are usually conducted by a bishop.

FOR YOUR FOLDERS

▶ Explain what Christians think about baptism.
▶ Look up Matthew 28:19–20, and copy the passage.
▶ Describe in your own words a Baptist baptismal service.
▶ Explain the New Testament teachings on baptism.

Baptism is seen as being the gateway into membership of the Church

50 PRAYER I

Christians believe in a personal God

THINGS TO DO

▶ Look at these two prayers. What types of prayer do you think they are?

'Lord make us an instrument of thy peace,
where there is hatred, let us sow love;
where there is injury, pardon;
where there is discord, union;
where there is doubt, faith;
where there is despair, hope;
where there is darkness, light;
where there is sadness, joy;
for your mercy and for your truth's sake. Amen.'

(Prayer of St Francis)

'And in the name of every creature under heaven we too praise your glory as we say,
Holy, holy, holy Lord, God of power and might,
heaven and earth are full of your glory.
Hosanna in the highest.'

(from the *Roman Catholic Sunday Missal*)

Most Christians practise private prayer, believing that they find their closest experience of God in prayer. They believe that God is a *personal* God and that through prayer they can meet God. Here are some of the types of prayer used by Christians:

- **Adoration** – the person praying thinks about God's greatness, power, wisdom and love.
- **Confession** – when confronting the power of God's love the person praying becomes aware of their own weaknesses and may ask God for forgiveness.
- **Intercession** – 'intercede' means 'speak in favour of somebody'. As well as asking for God's forgiveness, the person praying may become aware of the needs of others. They may pray for the sick, the poor, the lonely or for people who are close to them or for the whole world.
- **Petition** – this is when the person praying makes a request to God for help.
- **Thanksgiving** – this form of prayer expresses thanks to God and praises God for His love.

Most Christian prayers are addressed to God, and they end with the words 'through Jesus Christ our Lord'. This is because many Christians believe that God is too great to approach directly and it is only through Jesus that they can approach Him. This is why Jesus is sometimes referred to as an 'advocate' or 'intercessor', a mediator between God and humanity. Protestant Christians believe that Jesus Christ is the only one who can mediate between them and God. Some Christians, like Roman Catholics, believe that others, like Mary the Mother of God or the Saints, can act as mediators.

Christians do not all pray in the same way. Some pray at regular times, others don't; some use their own words whilst others use set forms of prayer; some attach more importance to praying alone, others to praying communally (with others). Some Christians use another form of prayer called **contemplation** (see unit 20). This is a quiet form of prayer.

REFLECTION

'Christ realized the value of silence in prayer. He understood that God exists in every asepct of life and He knew that communication with God (who speaks through "the still small voice") is achieved through silent prayer. So we take time, even a few minutes, each day to assess our life relationship with God. We need to stop our minds jumping about. We need silence, a quietness, which brings its own peace. In such silence we discover life's goodness coming to us and we realize the futility of rushing after everything we think life has to offer.'
(The Reverend Canon A.J. Prescott, The Additional Curates Society Magazine, Advent 1988)

THINKING POINT

- **'Instead of supposing that one great God is thinking about the answer to millions of different problems of all the individuals in the world, is it not more reasonable to suppose that some action is set in motion by prayer which gives us the answer from our subconscious minds? In saying this I'm not saying that God doesn't exist. I'm saying that it might well be that this uplifting power somehow activates the subconscious solution-providing mechanism which would otherwise not be possible.'**
(Alistair Hardy, *The Divine Flame*, Religious Experience Research Unit 1966)

FOR YOUR FOLDERS

- ▶ Explain in your own words the different types of prayer used by Christians.
- ▶ Explain the meanings of these words: advocate; intercessor; mediator. How do Protestant and Roman Catholic views on the idea of a mediator differ?
- ▶ Explain what is meant by 'contemplation'.
- ▶ Why, according to Reverend Prescott, is silence important in Christian prayer?

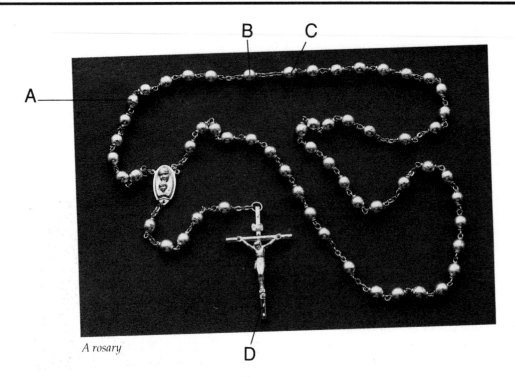

A rosary

Many Christians use the Bible, the rosary, the crucifix and icons to help them in their prayers.

The Bible

The Rosary

Many Roman Catholic Christians use a rosary when they are praying. A rosary is made up of five sets of ten beads. Each set of beads is called a 'decade' (A); each decade is separated by a bead which is more spaced out than the others (B). By counting the beads as they pray, Roman Catholics are able to contemplate some of the central events in the lives of Jesus and Mary. At each bead the person praying repeats the 'Ave Maria':

'Hail Mary, full of grace,
The Lord is with you.
Blessed are you among women
and blessed is the fruit of your womb, Jesus.
Holy Mary, Mother of God,
Pray for us sinners now
and at the hour of our death. Amen.'

At the first bead of the decade (C) the **Pater Noster** ('Our Father . . .', see opposite) is said. At the last bead of the decade the person will say the 'Gloria Patri':

'Glory be to the Father and to the Son and to the Holy Spirit, as it was in the beginning is now and ever shall be, world without end. Amen.'

The Crucifix

Hanging from the string of beads is a crucifix (D) (a cross with an image of Jesus on it), and five more beads. These beads represent a Pater Noster, three Ave Marias and a Gloria. When the person comes to the crucifix they say the Apostles' Creed (see unit 9). As well as being parts of rosaries, crucifixes can also be worn. They may also be statues.

Icons

(See photograph.) Icons are very important for Orthodox Christian prayer. Icons are religious paintings of Jesus, Mary, the Saints and angels. They are usually richly decorated. They are not simply portraits of people; they are intended to express their inner characters. It is the meaning behind the picture that is important. Orthodox Christians treat icons with great reverence and offer devotion to them. They are not praying to the icons, but rather using the icons as a means of offering prayers to God.

The Lord's Prayer

In the New Testament Jesus tells his disciples *'This is how you should pray'*, and gives them a prayer which is known as the Lord's Prayer. The Lord's Prayer is used by all Christian denominations and is the most important prayer in Christianity. Within this prayer are many different types of prayer:

The Mother of God icon

'Our Father in heaven, thy name be hallowed; thy kingdom come, thy will be done, on earth as in heaven. Give us today our daily bread.	This is an example of *adoration*. This is an example of *supplication*, or *humble petition*, for God to do something. In this case it expresses (a) the hope that God will bring to completion the salvation of the world, and (b) that He will provide for humanity.
Forgive us the wrong we have done, as we have forgiven those who have wronged us. And do not bring us to the test, but save us from the evil one.' (Matthew 6:9–13)	This is an example of a *penitential* prayer, i.e. asking God for forgiveness (**repentence**), and also recognizing that the person who is asking must also be prepared to forgive others. It is followed by a request for strength to try to avoid sinning in the future.

KEY WORDS

Doxology – this is a formula, usually used at the end of a prayer, praising God,

e.g. *'For thine is the kingdom, the power and the glory, for ever and ever. Amen.'*.

Amen – a word which means 'Let it be'.

FOR YOUR FOLDERS

▶ Write an essay of about 100 words on the way that Christians use the Bible, the rosary, the crucifix and icons to help them in their prayers.

▶ What sorts of prayers are to be found in the Lord's Prayer?

52 PILGRIMAGE

A 'pilgrimage' is literally a 'journey to a holy place'. It can also refer to our journey through life, or a journey inwards.

In Europe there are many places which became famous centres of pilgrimage, especially in the Middle Ages. *Santiago de Compostela* in Spain has been visited by pilgrims ever since the ninth century, because it is traditionally the site of the grave of the Apostle James. *Rome* in Italy is an important place of pilgrimage because of its many associations, particularly with the early Church. Many Roman Catholics like to visit the Vatican Palace, the home of the Pope, especially at festival times when the Pope blesses the crowd assembled in St Peter's Square.

In Britain the most famous place of pilgrimage is the shrine of St Thomas à Becket in *Canterbury* cathedral. *Walsingham* in Norfolk is an important centre for both Anglican and Roman Catholic Christians; a shrine was built there to the Virgin Mary in the eleventh century. Annual pilgrimages take place too, to St Cuthbert's tomb in *Durham* cathedral, to *Lindisfarne* (Holy Island) off the coast of Northumberland, and to *Iona*, an island off the coast of Scotland (see unit 30).

Modern pilgrims visit these and other holy places to pray and seek for spiritual guidance and refreshment. There are two places in particular that have become important places of pilgrimage for the sick, *Knock* in Ireland and *Lourdes* in France. In both places visions of the Virgin Mary were reported last century and the places are believed by many to have miraculous healing powers.

For many Christians the most important place of pilgrimage is the Holy Land, *Palestine* (called Israel today), the country where Jesus spent his earthly life.

Lourdes, in France – a place of pilgrimage for the sick

REFLECTION

'For me a pilgrimage should be a learning experience. It should deepen one's faith and also make one become aware of one's place in God's created world. My pilgrimage to Palestine did all of these things.

Sitting by the Sea of Galilee, the place where Jesus spent so much of his life, teaching and healing, I felt that he was in some way still there. The waters lapping gently against the shore and the warm breeze from the hills of the Lebanon, seemed to carry his eternal words. I felt a stillness inside and realized that a true pilgrimage is really a journey within – to that quiet still voice that lies deep inside each one of us. For me, the peace of that place had a depth and a presence that lies beyond words.

Jerusalem – the holiest of cities. Timeless. The narrow streets, the beggars, the fruit sellers, the small scuttling children, the donkeys laden with their wares, the soldiers wary and heavily armed. All not so very different from the time our Lord walked this city all those centuries ago. We walk carrying a cross on the Via Dolorosa – the Way of the Cross – following the steps of the Master when he was led to the Place of a Skull. We celebrate Mass – a truly holy experience in this sacred place.

The Garden of Gethsemane at night. The place where Jesus wept blood before his arrest. The trees, over 2000 years old, sway gently in the night air. A place of sadness and fear. I half expect to see a group of armed Roman soldiers coming for the man from Nazareth. A dog barks and a can of coke blows across the road. Haunting. I pray.

Bethlehem. There is a fear here not unlike the fear in Herod's day. A curfew has been called – the streets are deserted. In the last few months over 300 Palestinians have been killed by the Israeli army. Yesterday a three-year-old girl was shot dead in the street of Bethlehem. How little has changed, it seems, from the day when the Prince of Peace was born in the little stable across the road. An ornate star marks the place of His birth in a church now full of guides and tourists and guarded by a young Israeli soldier. Christ himself was a Palestinian Jew and I wonder if He returned today where He would be and what He would say? The Christ of the oppressed and the downtrodden. The Christ who said, "Blessed are the peacemakers." I weep and pray to God that one day there will be peace and justice in this land, in this world and in all our hearts.

My pilgrimage was sad, beautiful and moving. I learnt that if we have faith God will guide us through this life. I became aware of the timelessness of Christ's message to the world and of the eternal truth of His words. I realized that the stories in the Gospels did not happen in a vacuum, but in a real land with real people. A beautiful land. A land of synagogues, mosques and churches. A land of deserts, of staggeringly beautiful sunsets, of palm leaves and dusty roads'.

(Joan Turner, a Roman Catholic, author's interview)

TALKING POINT

- 'For me a pilgrimage should be a learning experience. It should deepen one's faith and also make one become aware of one's place in God's created world.'

FOR YOUR FOLDERS

► Find an atlas and draw a map of the world. Mark some places of Christian pilgrimage on it.

► *'A true pilgrimage is really a journey within.'* Explain what you think this means. Try and describe in your own words some of the feelings and emotions that Joan Turner experienced on her pilgrimage.

In 1986 Satish Kumar went on a walking pilgrimage to the holy places of Britain. He had no money and stayed with people on the way.

REFLECTION

'My plan was to start at nine o'clock in the morning and to arrive at my host's house between 4 pm and 6 pm in the evening. With a few exceptions I aimed at walking every day, covering 20 miles per day on average. I started out with a small rucksack with one change of clothes. I took no book, no diary, no camera, no money. Pilgrimage is best if you are travelling light, especially if you are walking.

Why, O why are a pilgrim's legs lacking in strength? I had been living in a world of motorized transport. I had lost touch with walking but I was glad to be back on my feet and rediscovering the pain and pleasure of walking on my own two legs.

The tradition of going on a pilgrimage is common to all religions. The Muslims go to Mecca, the Christians go to Canterbury or Jerusalem, and Hindus go to the source of the River Ganges in the Himalayas. So pilgrims' routes are established all over the world and it was a great delight to walk the ancient path to Canterbury.

In India before you enter a temple, you go round it, to leave your negative thoughts behind. When your body, mind and heart are ready, then you may enter the temple. Similarly I make a journey around the temple of Britain, so that I may enter into its mysteries.

This pilgrimage is a pilgrimage to Britain, to its rivers, hills, moors, dales, fields, to all its natural beauty. Walking every day will take me four months. In India I knew four women who walked all over India, taking 12 years.

In Canterbury Cathedral there is an area designated for private prayer and meditation where pilgrims light a candle. In this dark corner of the Cathedral, lit only by the many candles, I too lit a candle and said the Prayer for Peace. After giving his blessings Canon Brett led me to the chapel of Thomas à Becket. Although modernized the chapel has an atmosphere of martyrdom, the sword hanging above the altar spoke the language of power and pain. I stood in silence and astonishment as Canon Brett told me the story: the Archbishop knew that the Knights were coming to kill him. His monks urged him to escape or to order them to resist. The Archbishop calmly said, "Why should I hide? I am not afraid of death. One thing is certain: all of us will die one day, no need to escape or hide. As for resistance, we are not here to resist but to suffer. We will not take life, we will offer life." And so Thomas à Becket died at the altar and became a martyr.

The King had wanted to break the power of the Church and so had appointed his friend Thomas à Becket the Archbishop of Canterbury. But when Thomas took his place in Canterbury his inner voice told him that he must be true to God, and being true to God brought him into conflict with the church.

Ely Cathedral. Almost six miles before reaching this beautiful building I could see its outline. As I walked closer and closer, the grandeur of this magnificent holy place of pilgrimage slowly revealed itself. This day's walk felt easy. The river bank was soft and level but more than that I felt I was being pulled by the power of the Cathedral. By the time I arrived in Ely Cathedral I was already so much

'The tree is my church, my poem, my prayer'

immersed in the visual and emotional experience of the Cathedral I felt I knew it intimately.

There was no longer free entrance to this holy place and when I urged the box office clerk to let me, a penniless pilgrim, go and offer my prayers before the altar I was told that no exception could be made. As I looked inside at those holding their tickets, eating ice creams, treating the building as a historic monument, a museum, reading up on facts and figures, it seemed to me that spiritual experience was more easy outside than inside its walls.

Sometimes I came across a tree which seemed like a Buddha or a Jesus, loving, compassionate, unambitious, enlightened, in eternal meditation, giving pleasure to a pilgrim, shade to a cow, berries to a bird, beauty to its surroundings, health to its neighbours, branches for the fire, leaves to the soil, asking nothing in return, in total harmony with the wind and the rain. How much I can learn from a tree. The tree is my church, my temple, the tree is my poem and my prayer.

In the shrine of our Lady of Walsingham, I felt I was entering the womb of the mother goddess. The room is lit only by candles and as all pilgrims do I lit a candle. As I stood in silence, my eyes closed, I saw a white silhouette of a goddess against a grey background. The silhouette was not external, it rose from within. It was an expression of the power of the feminine. I came out of the womb room to the holy well of healing water. Thousands of pilgrims have come to drink this holy water and be healed. I drank. How it was special I could not tell but certainly it was no ordinary water. I could not leave Walsingham without visiting the Russian Orthodox worship. In an aura of calm and peace a pilgrim is effortlessly lifted into a state of prayer. Like walking by the river or in the woods the atmosphere of calmness helps to encourage inner stillness. The wonder of Walsingham is in its atmosphere of tranquillity.

My pilgrimage was a sort of penance. Penance is a process of cleansing the soul, undertaken entirely voluntarily. It's not a punishment or a penalty. In the course of our daily lives our bodies require cleansing, as in the course of constant speech we need a period of silence, as after the company of others we need a period of solitude, so after my years of worldly life I needed to perform an act that would nurture the soul. Being on the road is hard on the body but is a state in which the soul can take wings and the spirit can be free.'

(Satish Kumar, Resurgence 119, November/December 1986)

FOR YOUR FOLDERS

▶ Explain in your own words what this pilgrimage around Britain meant for Satish Kumar, and the feelings, emotions and thoughts that he experienced.

▶ Briefly explain why Thomas à Becket is regarded as being a martyr.

▶ For Satish a pilgrimage is more than just visiting holy places. Explain why this is so.

KEY WORDS

Ethics – 'Ethics are concerned with rules of conduct, with the difference between right and wrong, good and bad. Morality has the same meaning, and the two words are more or less interchangeable. The word "ethics" comes from Greek and "morality" from Latin, and originally they both meant customs and habits. Ethics and morals, however, are not concerned merely with what people do, but with what is generally accepted they should, must, ought to do, regardless of whether or not they actually do it.'

Social ethics – 'The ethics of society itself which are concerned mainly with the conduct of groups of people, of society as a whole, of nations and the world community; with how they behave to other groups, other societies and nations, to animals and the natural world, and of course to the individual, man, woman, or child.'

Individual ethics – 'The ethical standards we learn from childhood on, and which most of us normally abide by . . . the rules which comprise our in-built private morality . . . the distinction between social and individual ethics is frequently blurred . . . in one sense all ethics are social.'

(John St John, *Religion and Social Justice*, Pergamon Press 1985)

As the dominant religion in western Europe, Christianity has had a major influence on social ethics and has itself been influenced by the continually changing world. Often the state has looked to the Church for ethical guidance. Also, the Church has often become part of the political system and upheld the authority of the state, though this has often meant it agreeing with policies which are 'unChristian'. The Church has sometimes compromised its ethical teachings in the face of the harsh reality of the world. A recent example was the Anglican Church's attitude to the Falklands War (1982). Look carefully at these two statements:

'War as a method of settling international disputes is incompatible with the teaching and example of our Lord Jesus Christ. The use of the modern technology of war is the most striking example of corporate sin and the prostitution of God's gifts.'

(Lambeth Conference 1978)

'In this world, to have done nothing, to have turned the other cheek, meant that we should have been accomplices in making the world an even less stable place . . . As Christians we can only regard war as evil. The only justification for the use of force as a last resort is to provide breathing space for moral ideas and truths to be established.'

(Sermon by the Archbishop of Canterbury 1982)

In this statement in 1982, the Archbishop was admitting that in a particular crisis, in the real world, the teachings of Christ are very difficult to apply.

Hector Peterson aged ten shot dead by police in South Africa, which claims to be a Christian country

Although many Christians in the past have used the teachings in the Bible to attack injustices, selected passages have often been used to justify unethical policies, like religious wars, slavery and anti-Semitism. The self-interest and greed that seem to motivate a free capitalist market economy, as we have in western Europe, hardly fit in with the teaching of Jesus about selflessness and generosity. It can be argued, however, that Jesus' teachings were set against a world that was very different from our own, and so it is perhaps impossible to draw exact parallels with our modern world. However, many Christians would say that the teachings in the Gospels are relevant today, because their message is eternal.

In the next few units we shall be looking at some of the most important social issues facing the human race, and the views of individual Christians and of the Churches.

THINKING POINT

- 'It's no good saying Christ's teachings are not valid in the world. The fact is they are not valid because the Church has never had the courage to put them into practice.'

TALKING POINTS

- 'The study of social ethics includes many of the most important and difficult issues of our day. Christian responses to them have often been confused, contradictory, hesitant, ill-informed, and subject to bitter attacks from both inside and outside the Churches.'

    (Archbishop of York)

- 'A religion true to its nature must also be concerned about man's social conditions. Religions deal with both heaven and earth, both time and eternity. Religion operates not only on the vertical plane but also on the horizontal. It seeks not only to integrate men with God but to integrate men with men and each man with himself. This means that the Christian gospel is a two-way road. On the one hand it seeks to change the souls of men and thereby unite them with God; on the other hand, it seeks to change the environmental conditions of men so that the soul will have a chance after it is changed. Any religion that professes to be concerned with the souls of men and is not concerned with the slums that damn them, the economic conditions that strangle them, and the social conditions that cripple them, is a dry-as-dust religion. Such a religion is the kind Marxists like to see – an opiate of the people.'

    (Martin Luther King)

FOR DISCUSSION

▶ 'There is no social evil, no form of injustice which has not been sanctified in some way or another by religious sentiment.'

    (Reinhold Niebuhr)

▶ 'Christianity has supported and sometimes created institutions which deny individuals even a limited opportunity to dispose of their lives with at least something like the same freedom as others in the same society.'

    (John Bowker)

FOR YOUR FOLDERS

▶ Can you think of some policies followed by governments that are without doubt 'unChristian'?

▶ How did the Anglican Church compromise its views when discussing the Falklands War? How did it try to justify this compromise?

▶ Do you think that it is true to say that the Church has failed to live up to Christ's teachings? What are the views of Reinhold Niebuhr and John Bowker?

Ivan Toms (right) speaks to Charles Bester after the court hearing

In 1982, London Weekend Television conducted a poll among the Anglican clergy. Briefly, its findings were that a sizeable number of clergy polled believed that they should concern themselves not only with the spiritual life of the people under their care, but also with improving the economic and social environment in which they live; and that leading churchmen should speak out against government policies to which they were opposed.

This poll reflects a growing debate in Britain, and indeed worldwide, about the role of the Church regarding political issues. This debate is often the cause of much controversy. In Britain, for instance, many bishops have spoken out against what they believe to be the Conservative Government's divisive and unjust policies. In many ways this is ironic, because in the past the Church of England has been called 'the Tory party at prayer'.

REFLECTIONS

'However devoted were many of its ministers, however valuable their service, it was inescapably a rich man's Church. It was endowed with great wealth . . . its priests tended to be those who had been recruited from one class in society.'
  (G. Kitson Clark, Churchmen and the Condition of England, Methuen 1971)

'Human history is a process of growth. Almost every religion in one way or another includes in its story the dream of the journey. Where this is denied, there are danger signals that what was meant to be liberating is becoming an imprisonment and that human anxiety is hijacking the one resource which makes fresh movement and discovery possible.'
  (Michael Duke)

'Prayer and contemplation, in established religion, become purely private practices within a social order which they neither question nor threaten. Religion has become privatized. Not only that, private religions have become a multi-million dollar industry. They are part of capitalism's success story – religions as commodities, religions which in no way threaten or disturb social stability.'
  (Kenneth Leech, The Social God, Sheldon 1981)

There are times when many individual Christians' consciences lead them into confrontation with governments. Sometimes Christians who have a deeply held conviction may find themselves in a situation which challenges their faith and may lead them into direct conflict with the authorities. This newspaper article illustrates such a case.

Youth who defied SA army is jailed

SOUTH AFRICA'S youngest conscientious objector, a committed Christian, was jailed yesterday for six years for refusing to do military service.

Pandemonium erupted in the Johannesburg Magistrates' Court as Charles Bester, 18, was given the maximum sentence. About 100 supporters, including members of his family, broke into chants of "Viva" and then sang South Africa's "alternative" national anthem, "Nkosi, sikelele Afrika" ("God bless Africa"). The magistrate ordered the court doors shut and all those in the public gallery, including several priests, were led to the cells. They were freed after a few minutes.

Mr Bester, who pleaded not guilty, turned to his sympathisers after the sentence had been read. "Thanks for your support," he said. "You shall know the truth and the truth shall set you free." Earlier, he told the court that his Christian conscience prevented him from participating in "the evil" perpetuated by the South African Defence Force. "We desperately need reconciliation to come together and find out about each other," he said, adding that apartheid, which the SADF upheld, caused untold suffering and humiliation.

Ursula Bruce, the mother of David Bruce, 26, who received the same sentence in July, was in court, as was Ivan Toms, who was released on bail last week after serving nine months of a two-year sentence for

From Christopher Gilbert
in Johannesburg

refusing to attend an army camp. Dr Toms has been granted an appeal. At least two of the 143 young men who publicly announced in August that they would not serve in the SADF, were also present to show their solidarity.

The Pretoria government, however, is equally determined to bring the full force of the law to bear in such cases, and Mr Bester's tender years quite clearly left the magistrate unmoved. Pretoria has long been concerned about the dangers to morale implicit in such acts of defiance — and 1988 has been an especially difficult year. After the publicity generated at home and abroad by the Bruce case and that of the 143, the End Conscription Campaign — which co-ordinated "draft-dodging" activities — was banned.

All white able-bodied men over the age of 17 have to do two years' national service followed by a further 24 months' service spread over the next 12 years. Reacting to yesterday's events in Johannesburg, the Charles Bester Support Group released a statement deeply regretting that "the state has seen fit to impose this maximum sentence". Mr Bester's "religious conviction, his sincerity of faith, his integrity of conscience . . . have inspired all who heard him during his defence. His vision for a new South Africa will one day prevail".

(Independent,
6 December 1988)

FOR YOUR FOLDERS

▶ After reading the three reflections, try to describe in your own words what each one is saying.

▶ Read the newspaper article and explain why Charles Bester went to prison for six years (see unit 63 for more background).

! ▶ Do you think that the Church and individual Christians should get involved in politics?

TALKING POINT

● 'The church must say to worldly rulers, whose laws are at variance with the laws of God, "We had much rather obey God than man"' (Acts 4:19).

(Archbishop Desmond Tutu)

Britain Today

1 Over one million dwellings are considered unfit to live in.
2 More than 100000 families are officially recognized as homeless.
3 An estimated sixteen million people (29 per cent of the population) are living in poverty or on its margins; two million of them are children. This represents a rise of 33 per cent since 1979.
4 Unemployment among black people is double that among white people.
5 In 1986 571 elderly people died of hypothermia in their homes.
6 Five per cent of the population own 40 per cent of the nation's wealth.
7 The National Health Service is suffering from lack of funds and resources whilst the Trident nuclear submarine programme is costing over £10 billion – the same as 500 new hospitals.

No YTS, no money, is now the rule for 90,000 youngsters. Edward Pilkington reports

CHRIS from Birmingham is down on his luck. He pulls a few pounds from the pocket of his ripped leather jacket. That will tide him over till the end of the week, then he will be back on the scrounge. Two weeks ago he had his last remaining source of legitimate income cut off. Now he does his best to make ends meet from day to day. "I don't think I can survive for long like this," he says, adding nonchalantly: "I suppose I'll have to think of something else."

Chris does not look, talk or act like the stereotype of the wide-eyed and bushy-tailed 17-year-old. He left school two years ago and has been living off state benefits ever since.

Though he would like a job, employers will not take him because they dislike his punky clothes and hair gelled into the shape of a trident.

This year Chris's fortunes have gone from bad to worse. In April his benefits were cut with the introduction of income support from £30 to £19 a week, and again to £15 in September. Now even that paltry amount has been entirely withdrawn. On November 7 he drew his final Giro, which was meant to last for two weeks but didn't. Now Chris will have to leave home because his father cannot support him; and because he is no longer in receipt of benefits no hostel for the homeless will take him. Which leaves him with no money, no job, no home.

(*Guardian*, 23 November 1988)

Charities

Some people believe that charities are good in that they help people to help each other and be more caring. However, many people believe that in a true welfare state charities should not be needed, and the government has a responsibility to help the needy.

In the second half of the nineteenth century, many social reformers, often Christians, began setting up homes and orphanages for the poor. The work of charities had begun. In 1905 the Liberal Party introduced a wide range of social services which later developed into the welfare state. The state became responsible for helping the poor. However, today, because of government policies, more and more pressure is being put on charitable organizations as the numbers of poor increase. Poverty gives rise to a whole range of personal and social pressures and problems, such as drug addiction, alcohol abuse, crime, violence, prostitution and depression.

Increasingly the Churches in Britain are beginning to attack many of the policies of the Government. They question the morality of a society that values materialism, competition, free market forces, a reduced welfare state, consumerism and lack of resources for hospitals and schools and for the more vulnerable members of society. In 1985 the Church of England published a report called 'Faith in the City' which condemned the terrible poverty and bleak environments that millions of people have to endure in the urban priority areas.

REFLECTION

'The Churches in Britain have enormous wealth. Indeed the Church represents one of the wealthiest sectors of society. Yet you can walk around any city in Britain today and find people who have to sleep on the streets while the Church doors are locked. While young people are hassled on the streets by pimps, police officers and drug pushers, the Churches lie silent like empty tombs. While the bishops live in palaces and the clergy in spacious vicarages, the poor live in rat infested damp hovels or on the street. The Church has lost its way. Jesus said "Sell your possessions and give to the poor". The Church has its possessions. It locks them up at night while the

poor struggle to live. Is this true Christianity? I don't think so. When Jesus saw the hypocrisy and the materialism of the Temple in Jerusalem, he turned the tables over. I have no doubt that he'd do the same thing in Britain today if he saw the state of the Church. Christianity to be true to its teaching, cannot compromise in any way. The Churches should be out there on the streets. The Churches should be demanding and protesting against what is going on in this country. The Churches should open their doors and keep them open, so that people can meet there, talk there, share their problems with others, sleep, dance, eat and drink in an atmosphere of tolerance and friendship. They should be places where people can learn how to become active and press for a better quality of life. But, alas, the Church in many places in Britain has become an empty tomb full of symbols that mean nothing to the people.'

(Billy Lucas, Youth and Community worker, author's interview)

FOR YOUR FOLDERS

▶ Using some of the statistics given in this unit design a poster with the theme 'Poverty in Britain today'.

▶ How can charities be abused by governments?

▶ 'Charity begins at home.' Comment on this statement.

▶ Do you think the Churches can begin to tackle the problems of poverty? If so how?

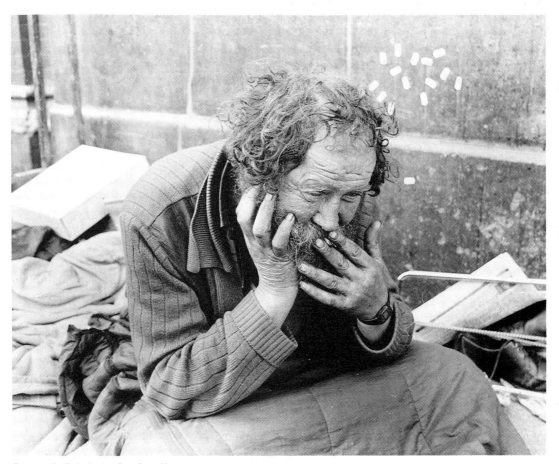

Poverty in Britain is a harsh reality

57 WORK I

'The worst evil is that the unemployed feel they are not wanted'

What is work?

Work is part of living and doing the things that are essential to stay alive. It is an activity natural to people. But not all human activity is work of this sort. Some of it is play or rest, and some of it involves using the mind. For many people work is what they get paid for, though often people do not stop working when they are not paid for it. Work has been described as 'purposeful activity'. In this unit we shall be looking at some Christian attitudes to work, unemployment and leisure.

Six aspects of work?

1 WORK IS NECESSARY

It is first of all necessary for human survival. The idea of work as being necessary for human survival is reflected in the Bible:

> *'The Lord God took the man and put him in the garden of Eden to till it and care for it.'*
>
> (Genesis 2:15)

2 WORK IS CREATIVE

By mastering the elements of nature, humans are able to create things. Adam and Eve are told to:

> *'Be fruitful and increase, fill the earth and subdue it.'*
>
> (Genesis 1:28)

This shows human beings being creative and exercising control, sharing with God in the further development of his creation.

> *'Work is a good thing . . . through work man not only transforms nature, adapting it to his own needs, but he also achieves fulfilment as a human being and, indeed, in a sense, becomes more a human being.'*
>
> ('The Teachings of Pope John Paul II', *Human Work*, Catholic Truth Society 1982)

3 WORK IS PAINFUL

Work can be hard, back-breaking, repetitive, boring, meaningless and soul-destroying. It can lead to mental and physical illness and sometimes even to death.

> *'The work is external to the worker – he does not fulfil himself in work . . . has a feeling of misery . . . is physically and mentally debased.'*
>
> (Karl Marx 1818–1883)

4 WORK IS HEALTHY

Work brings us into relationship with other people. It helps people belong to a community, by giving them a place, status, belonging and value. It is vital for people's mental and spiritual health.

5 WORK IS GOOD

Work is a way of obtaining the necessities of life. Some Christians believe that work is a means of sharing with God in being creative in this world.

During the Industrial Revolution in the nineteenth century, work to some Christians, especially Protestant Christians, became a sort of religious duty. Hard work was seen as being a virtue. This idea became known as the 'Protestant work ethic'.

6 WORK IS A VOCATION

Some Christians believe that they have a 'calling' from God to do certain sorts of work.

'A vocation means that we see what we do, as an expression of our faith and a response to God's love for us.'

(*What does Methodism Think? 1980*)

Some jobs that are recognized as 'callings' might include the priesthood, nursing, teaching, social work, etc.

Unemployment

In many parts of the world people cannot find work. There are many reasons for this, and the Christian Churches are only too aware of the personal and social problems that unemployment can cause.

'The worst evil, in the sense that the unemployed feel that they have fallen out of the common life . . . they are not wanted. That is the thing that has the power to corrupt the soul of any man.'

(William Temple)

Leisure

Leisure time is generally on the increase in our society. Most Christians believe that leisure time should be used constructively so that people become rested and fulfilled.

'Leisure is good if used for the glory of God.'
(Methodist Conference 1974)

Traditionally, Sunday has been a day of rest in our society. However, this is not so much the case today, e.g. more shops are opening on a Sunday:

'Every society needs a day of rest and 'Re-creation', such as the Christian Sunday has provided.'
(Church of England Board of Social Responsibility Report 1985)

FOR YOUR FOLDERS

▶ Give an outline of the six aspects of work.
▶ In what ways might Christians' beliefs affect:
  a the type of jobs they do
  b their attitudes to work
▶ How might Christians try to spend their leisure time?
▶ What do you think are the personal and social costs of unemployment? How might the Churches help unemployed people?

FOR DISCUSSION

▶ 'Everyone has the right to work and to just and favourable conditions of employment. Everyone has the right to equal pay for equal work. Everyone has the right to form and join a trades union. Everyone has the right to rest and leisure, including reasonable working hours and holidays with pay.'
(UN Declaration of Human Rights)

People who hold strong religious beliefs often find that their faith affects and is affected by every aspect of their daily lives and work. Christians find themselves in many different types of work. Sometimes this work can be very demanding, can involve enormous stress and be emotionally draining. In this reflection a social worker working in a child protection team in the inner city talks about her work.

REFLECTION

'The whole of my working life involves me in dealing with children who have been physically or sexually abused or neglected or have experienced any combination of these horrors. It was because of my own Christian beliefs that I wanted to in some way help people. So I trained as a social worker. As a mother myself, and aware that children have rights not to be abused or exploited in any way, I found myself drawn to working with children.

The children I work with are in extreme distress and danger. Much has been made in the media recently of the Cleveland case which may make people think that the sexual abuse of children does not really happen in our society. It does happen. It happens to children of all ages. It happens to young babies. It happens to teenagers. I have interviewed young girls of fourteen who told me of the abuse starting when they were about six years old. I have also played with two-year-olds and become aware through that play that something very wrong was happening to them in their home, the one place where they should feel totally safe and secure.

It is at times both sad and desperate work. Desperate because when a young child starts to trust you, and tells you that his or her mother or father has done things to them that are a total betrayal of the trust rested in them, my first reaction is often one of anger. Anger that I must disguise from the child. It can be desperate and sad. At the end of a session I can feel drained, emotionally sapped dry. I think it is here that my faith gives me strength. In Mark's Gospel there is a story of a sick woman who, in a large crowd, secretly touched Christ's clothes, knowing it would heal her. Christ felt that some power had gone out of him and said. "My daughter, your faith has cured you." Christ experienced joy at the woman's faith. By giving he received her faith. By giving her faith, she received Christ's healing

powers. I believe that in life, if we truly give then we will receive.

It is my experience that with younger children, if the father has been the abuser, the mother can be encouraged and supported to provide for her child an environment safe from risk of further abuse. Sadly this is often not so with girls of twelve upwards. All too often these young teenagers tell somebody what

Physical abuse happens to children of all ages

is happening in the hope of support from the non-abusing parent. All too frequently they find that it is they, not the abuser, who lose their family and hope for a secure and loving future.

Sadly child sexual abuse, by its very nature as a "secret, hidden" crime is far more difficult to deal with than the physical abuse of children. But the physical abuse of children can be particularly frightening to deal with as sometimes a child dies, and social workers are once again on the front page of every newspaper.

Working in this area is very demanding, but it has its rewards. For example, when you do sometimes get a family that changes and the child can grow up in an atmosphere where the affection doesn't any more become distorted. Sometimes the parents need enormous help and support before they are able to take on their responsibilities.

However difficult and harrowing I sometimes find this work, I feel that its basis for me is in Jesus' own very apparent love for children:

"Jesus called for the children and said, 'Let the little ones come to me; do not try to stop them; for the kingdom of God belongs to such as these.'"

(Luke 18:15, 16)

Jesus would wish that all children lead happy, secure and fulfilled lives; so do I.'

(Elizabeth Turner, author's interview)

THINKING POINT

- 'It has been said that a society should be judged by the way it treats its weakest and most vulnerable members. If this is so then our society has to be declared guilty. But why do people resort to such brutal behaviour? What makes men and women abuse children? There can be little doubt that we live in an increasingly violent society. The root causes of violence are many. Television is full of violent programmes. Newspapers and magazines revel in telling us 'horror stories'. All of them affect and influence people. Many people are frustrated in their lives, they feel lost and hopeless. Tragically children often bear the brunt of their frustrations. As a society we need to begin to look seriously and critically at the way the media influences people and also to consider why so many people should feel frustrated in their lives.'

THINGS TO DO

▶ Try to find someone in your community whose religious faith inspires and helps them in their work. Try to arrange a time when you can interview them. Take a cassette recorder along with you.

FOR YOUR FOLDERS

▶ Describe in your own words why Elizabeth's work is often difficult and harrowing.
▶ Why do you think child sexual abuse is a 'hidden, secret' crime?
▶ How does Elizabeth's faith help her in her work?

9 'GOD MADE THEM MALE AND FEMALE'

Throughout human history, societies have been ruled and dominated by men. Often in the past women had no status. History, culture, language and religion have been patriarchal. Even in the Bible, particularly in the teaching of St Paul, women were viewed as being second-class citizens:

'I permit no woman to teach or to have authority over men.'   (1 Timothy 2:12)

However, in the twentieth century women have been able to influence western society and demand equal rights and status.

Like all other **patriarchal** institutions, the Church has been guilty of **sexism**. Even today sexist attitudes still exist in many Churches and among many 'Churchmen'. Over the last few years a new force has arisen in the Christian Church, which is sometimes called 'female theology'. Feminists (women who actively struggle for the principle that women should have the same rights and chances as men) have begun to make the Church think again about its patriarchical organizations, its male-dominated language and its sexist attitudes.

KEY WORDS

Sexism – 'the opinion that one sex is not as good as another; especially that women are less able in most ways than men.'
Patriarchy – 'a social group or system ruled or controlled by men.'
(*Longman's Dictionary of Contemporary English*)

Women Priests

A debate is raging within the Anglican Church about whether the Church should allow women priests to be fully ordained. In Canada, New Zealand and the USA, women can become priests, but in Britain they can only become deacons. There are more than 1200 women priests in the Anglican Church worldwide and one woman bishop in the USA. These numbers are growing. In this reflection an American woman priest gives her opinion about this controversial subject.

REFLECTION

'The women's movement has already made sizeable inroads into male supremacy, which, apart from inertia, employs ridicule as a means of counter-attack. Nowhere are males more firmly entrenched than in some of the Churches, particularly the Anglicans and Roman Catholics, though the as yet small group of Christian feminists is pressing them hard.

A remarkable parallel to the gains of the women's movement are the changes in the life of nuns: the convents have suffered something approaching a mass exodus but those who remain have insisted on radical reforms, including discarding medieval dress for shorter skirts and a simple veil, taking university degrees, joining in political demonstrations, rebelling against the hierarchical powers of male prelates and mothers superior, and much else. These reforms contrast with the continuing refusal of the Roman Catholic and the bulk of (British) Anglican clergy to agree to women's ordination. Many Christian women are fed up with being expected to change the church flowers, polish the altar brass and make the tea and cakes for social events while they are refused the right to more than a token participation in their Church's services. Only a male is considered suitable to bless and administer the

sacrament at Holy Communion, as if women were not 'made in God's image' too. Feminists also argue that without female priests God's nature is not fully presented to the world.

The growing acceptance that God must have feminine as well as masculine characteristics – or that He/She is sexless – is tied up with the whole question of what is meant by gender, apart from biological differences. To what extent do these differences determine personality and ability? What relative parts are played by one's sex-linked genetic inheritance and what by nurture and upbringing (e.g. dolls or toy soldiers; identification with the parent of the same sex; expectations at school, in the media, etc.)? The answers to these questions are complex and disputed, but there are plenty of familiar, stereotyped characteristics, whatever their source or inevitability, which are associated with gender and which society normally accepts and in practice enforces. The male is associated with doing, controlling, achieving, and with being rational, decisive, ambitious compared with the female, who is associated with nurturing comforting, submitting and being gentle, peaceful, irrational, intuitive.'
(*John St John, Religion and Social Justice, Pergamon Press 1985*)

The debate about women priests is raging within the Anglican Church

Dear Sirs · man to man · manpower · craftsman

working men · the thinking man · the man in the street

fellow countrymen · the history of mankind

one-man show · man in his wisdom · statesman

forefathers · masterful · masterpiece · old masters

the brotherhood of man · Liberty Equality Fraternity

sons of free men · faith of our fathers · god the father

god the son · yours fraternally · amen   words fail me

THINGS TO DO

▶ Explain why the words above are sexist. What alternative words are there?

REFLECTION

'At first I was rejected in my Church because I was black. Then I was rejected because I was a woman. The Church is controlled by men. It has been and still is guilty of sexism. There are many instances of women having considerable responsibility in the early Church. The Gospels, let us not forget, were all written by men in a period of history when women had few rights, so when people tell me that all Christ's disciples were men I say, "Of course it appears like that, because the Gospel writers were men living in a sexist world." Christ, however, is recorded as being very close to a number of women and he, tried to teach that everyone is equal. The language of the Church is sexist too. Why does it always convey a male God? Surely God, the creator of everything, is both male and female. As women we want to be consulted about attitudes in the Church and not be expected just to make cups of tea."
(Reverend Nan Peete, author's interview)

FOR YOUR FOLDERS

▶ Can you think of examples of sexism that are still prevalent in society today?

▶ Why do many feminists still 'view the Church as an enemy', according to John St John?

▶ How does Angela West argue that the 'Messiah' identified with women?

▶ What changes have taken place in convents?

▶ Can you think of some examples of the way that our society often stereotypes men and women?

! ▶ Look up the following in the Bible: 1 Timothy 2:12; 1 Corinthians 14:34, 35. People who argue against the ordination of women priests often use these passages to support their arguments. What are your views on this matter?

The rings are blessed and exchanged during a marriage service

The Christian religion sets a high value on marriage. The joining of a husband and wife in 'holy matrimony' is thought to relect the union of Christ with his followers. Christians believe that in their love for each other, married couples will experience and learn of God's love for His creation. In the Gospels, Jesus taught that God's purpose was that marriage should be a lifelong and intimate union.

> *'In the beginning, at the Creation, God made them male and female. For this reason a man shall leave his father and mother, and be made one with his wife; and the two shall become one flesh.'*
>
> (Mark 10:6–8)

The Church has recognized that not everyone is called to marriage, and has at times given a high value to celibacy. Generally Christians believe that there are three reasons for marriage:

- the right relationship for sexual intercourse;
- the procreation of children;
- the couple's mutual help and comfort in life.

In Britain, most Christians get married in a church service, although some may marry in a registry office. Here are some extracts from *A Roman Catholic Marriage Service* which show some of the beliefs and practices of Christian marriage.

Father, you have made the union of man and wife so holy a mystery
that it symbolizes the marriage of Christ and His Church.

Look with love upon this woman, your daughter, now joined to her husband in marriage.
She asks your blessing.
Give her the grace of peace and love.
May she always follow the example of the holy women whose praises are sung in the scriptures.
May her husband put his trust in her and recognize that she is his equal and the heir with him to the life of grace.
May he always honour her and love her as Christ loves His bride, the Church.
Father, keep them always true to Your commandments.
Keep them faithful in marriage and let them be living examples of Christian life.
Give them the strength which comes from the Gospel
so that they may be witnesses of Christ to others.
(Bless them with children and help them to be good parents. May they live to see their children's children.)
And after a happy old age,
grant them fulness of life with the saints in the kingdom of heaven.
We ask this through Jesus Christ our Lord.
Amen

Conclusion of the service.

All: (*The Lord's Prayer.*)

The final blessing.
The Dismissal.
The Civil Register (the couple, with witnesses, go to sign the civil register).

Bidding prayers.

Priest: *In the love of man and wife, God shows us a wonderful reflection of His own eternal love. Today N and N have dedicated themselves to one another in unending love. They will share with one another all that life brings. Let us ask God to bless them in the years ahead, and to be with them in all the circumstances of their marriage.*

Priest: *You have come together in this church so that the Lord may seal and strengthen your love in the presence of the church's minister and this community. Christ abundantly blesses this love. He has already **consecrated** you in baptism and now he enriches and strengthens you by a special sacrament so that you may assume the duties of a marriage in mutual and lasting fidelity . . . Are you ready freely and without reservation to give yourselves to each other in marriage?*

Couple: *I am (separately).*

Priest: *Are you ready to love and honour each other as man and wife for the rest of your lives? . . . NN, will you take NN here present for your lawful wife (husband), according to the rite of our Holy Mother the Church?*

Couple: *I will.*
I call upon these persons here present to witness that I NN, do take thee, NN, to be my lawful wedded wife (husband), to have and to hold from this day forward, for better for worse, for richer, for poorer, in sickness and in health, to love and to cherish, till death do us part.

Priest: *What God has joined together, let no man put . asunder.*
(*The rings are blessed and exchanged*)
May the Lord bless this ring (these rings) which you give (to each other) as the sign of your love and fidelity.
(*Bidding Prayers*)

All: *Hail Mary, full of grace, the Lord is with thee. Blessed art thou among women and blessed is the fruit of thy womb, Jesus Holy Mary Mother of God, pray for us sinners, now and at the hour of our death. Amen.*
(*The Nuptial Blessing*)

Priest: *Father by your power you have made everything out of nothing. In the beginning you created the universe and made mankind in your own likeness. You give man the constant help of woman so that man and woman should no longer be two, but one flesh, and you teach us that what you have united may never be divided.*
(Roman Catholic Marriage Service)

FOR YOUR FOLDERS

After reading though the extracts of a Roman Catholic marriage service answer the following questions.

▶ Use a dictionary to find out the meaning of the following words: consecrate; sacrament; fidelity; rite; cherish; asunder; nuptial.

▶ What do you think it means to 'honour' somebody?

▶ What do the couple promise in front of witnesses?

▶ Why do you think Roman Catholics have prayers about Mary? (See unit 15.)

▶ In the nuptial blessing are some major beliefs about God, Christ and the Church, and marriage. Write down what you think these beliefs are.

! ▶ What hopes about marriage are expressed in the nuptial blessing?

61 MARRIAGE II

A nuclear family

The family

The family is the basic social unit in most societies. It is the smallest and most common group in our society. Very generally, the family is made up of biologically related groups – parents and children living in a household; the group that someone grows up in. There are 'nuclear' families (where a couple live alone with their children, and no close relatives live in the household or neighbourhood) and 'extended' families (which consist of several generations, possibly living in the same household and having relatives in the neighbourhood). The organization and characteristics of the family may vary enormously, e.g. single-parent families, communes, step-parents, polygamy and so on.

In both the Old and New Testaments stress is put on the importance of the family and caring for members of the family. Pope John Paul II outlines some of the important characteristics of the family for Christians:

'The family is founded and given by love. It is a community of persons whose first task is to live with fidelity. Without love the family is not a community of persons and without love the family cannot live, grow and perfect itself as a community of persons.'
(Pope John Paul II)

Although some families are happy and closely knit, many are not. Indeed, even so-called 'happy families' have their problems. In our modern society there are many pressures on family life and tensions in the family can be caused by poverty, money worries, unemployment and changing roles, among other things.

Divorce

If a couple finds that they cannot live together there are three main solutions:

- **Desertion** – one partner simply leaves the other to live elsewhere.
- **Judicial** – the courts grant a separation, meaning the couple are not allowed in any way to interfere in each other's lives, and then after a period of time one partner can apply for a divorce without the consent of the other.
- **Divorce** – the marriage is officially declared by the courts to be at an end. After two years of living apart, and if both partners are willing, they may apply for a divorce.

Christian Churches have different views on divorce. Since 1966 the Church of England has taught that divorce is acceptable. The Roman Catholic Church's teaching is that in principle a marriage cannot be dissolved. However, there are some exceptions. The Roman Catholic Church can 'annul' a marriage. An 'annulment' is a declaration that the marriage bond did not exist. A marriage can be annulled if there is:

- a lack of consent (e.g. someone has been forced into marriage);
- a lack of judgement (e.g. if someone marries without being fully aware of what marriage entails);
- inability to carry out the duties of marriage (e.g. one partner may be mentally ill);
- a lack of intention (e.g. if one of the partners at the time of the marriage intends not to have any children while the other partner wants to have children).

REFLECTION

A Quaker view

'No couple, marrying with any deep conviction of permanence, would willingly give up the struggle to overcome their difficulties and seek a way of escape. But where the difficulties involved in a marriage are, of their very nature, serving to drive a couple further apart in bitterness of mind and heart, or when they reduce them to an empty and conventional semblance of living together, then there can be little reason for keeping within the bonds of legal marriage two people between whom no spiritual marriage exists.'

(The Quaker Home Service, Society of Friends 1949)

Birth control

Most couples in modern society feel the need to control the number of children they have. There are many different types of 'contraceptives' (methods by which couples can avoid an unwanted pregnancy). The Roman Catholic Church teaches that all artificial forms of contraception are wrong because the primary purpose of sexual intercourse is the begetting of children. The Catholic Church, however, does not condemn 'natural family planning' (NFP) which includes methods such as the woman becoming aware of her own fertile and infertile times by recording the natural signals of her body. The Catholic Church's teachings continue to raise much controversy, especially among some priests and nuns in the Third World where overpopulation is an enormous problem.

The Anglican view and the view of most Protestant churches is that couples may practise forms of contraception that are acceptable to both partners.

A Biblical love poem

The *Song of Songs* in the Bible is regarded by many people as being one of the most beautiful love poems ever written. Here are some excerpts:

Bridegroom

How beautiful you are, my dearest, how beautiful!
Your eyes behind your veil are like doves,
your hair like a flock of goats streaming down Mount Gilead.
Your teeth are like a flock of ewes just shorn
which have come up fresh from the dipping;
each ewe has twins and none has cast a lamb.
Your lips are like a scarlet thread,
and your words are delightful;
your parted lips behind your veil
are like a pomegranate cut open.
Your neck is like David's tower,
which is built with winding courses;
a thousand bucklers hang upon it,
and all are warriors' shields.
Your two breasts are like two fawns,
twin fawns of a gazelle.

(Song of Songs 4:1–7)

Bride

My beloved is fair and ruddy,
a paragon among ten thousand.
His head is gold, finest gold;
his locks are like palm-fronds.
His eyes are like doves beside brooks of water,
splashed by the milky water
as they sit where it is drawn.
His cheeks are like beds of spices or chests full of perfumes;
his lips are lilies, and drop liquid myrrh;
his hands are golden rods set in topaz;
his belly a plaque of ivory overlaid with lapis lazuli.

(Song of Songs 5:10–15)

FOR YOUR FOLDERS

▶ What is the Christian view on the nature and role of marriage and the family?
▶ What stresses do many families find themselves experiencing in modern society?
▶ Explain in your own words the Roman Catholic and Quaker views of divorce.
▶ Why has the Roman Catholic teaching on birth control caused controversy?

62 SEXUAL ETHICS

Sex is one of the most powerful human instincts and love is one of the most powerful human emotions. Because of the power of these instincts and emotions they often raise questions about right and wrong with regard to personal sexual behaviour, and questions about life and death.

For Christians living in the modern world these issues are of the utmost importance. Yet as we shall see they do not always agree.

In this unit we can only look at some of the key questions arising from sexual ethics. There are many more. After reading this unit discuss some of these issues.

KEY QUESTION

Should people have sex outside marriage?

'Every sexual act must be within the framework of marriage'

(Casti Conubii, *Catholic Encyclical*, Catholic Truth Society)

'If two mature people who are not married are deeply in love and are committed to each other in heart, body and soul, then yes, sexual intercourse as an expression of this love is acceptable.'

(Anglican priest)

KEY QUESTION

Should people be allowed to divorce?

'What God has joined together, man must not separate' (Mark 10:9)

'When the difficulties involved in a marriage are, of their very nature, serving to drive a couple further apart in bitterness of mind and heart or when they reduce them to an empty and conventional semblance of living together then there can be little reason for keeping within the bonds of legal marriage two people between whom no spiritual marriage exists.'

(*The Quaker Home Service*, Society of Friends 1949)

KEY QUESTION

Is abortion morally acceptable?

'If you do make a mistake, don't destroy the life . . . because also to that child God says: I have called you by your name, I have carved you in the palm of my hand: you are mine.'

(Mother Teresa)

'Although the foetus is to be specially respected and protected, nonetheless the life of the foetus is not absolutely sacrosanct if it endangers the life of the mother.'

(Church of England Board of Social Responsibility Report 1984)

KEY QUESTION

Is artificial insemination acceptable for couples who can't have children?

'Artificial insemination violates the dignity of the person and the sanctity of marriage. It is contrary to God's Law . . . a third party becoming involved in a marriage is like "mechanical adultery".'

(John Hardon, *Modern Catholic Dictionary*, Robert Hall 1980)

'Those engaging in artificial insemination are involved in a positive affirmation of the family. It is therefore regarded as an acceptable practice.'

(Church of England Report, 'Human Fertilization and Embryology' 1984)

KEY QUESTION

Is homosexuality morally acceptable?

'Homosexual acts are disordered and can in no case be approved of.'

(Roman Catholic Declaration of Sexual Ethics 1975)

'Homosexual acts are not wrong, since the quality of any homosexual relationship is . . . to be assessed the same way as a heterosexual relationship. For homosexual men and women, permanent relationships characterized by love can be an appropriate and Christian way of expressing their sexuality.'

(Methodist Conference 1979)

KEY QUESTION

Should Roman Catholic priests be celibate?

'Celibacy should be left to the free decision of the individual.'

(Hans Küng – theologian)

'Only by being celibate can I give myself totally to God.'

(A Catholic priest)

Love is one of the most powerful human emotions

(see unit 64)

KEY WORD

Racism – 'political and social practices based on differences between the races of people, and on the belief that one's own race is the best.'

(*Longman's Dictionary of Contemporary English*)

Racism and its prejudices have occupied a central place in world history. This century racism has been apparent in colonialism, in the apartheid system in South Africa (see unit 64) and in the ultimate horror of the Nazi holocaust during which the 'master race' exterminated some six million Jews plus huge numbers of victims from other 'inferior races'. While Britain has been relatively free from racial excesses, and gave shelter to thousands of Europe's refugees from the war, we cannot feel complacent. Racism still exists in society, though nowadays the victims are more likely to be black than Jewish. The last two decades have seen outbreaks of racial violence in our cities and opinion polls have shown that many white people have racist leanings, although they might not even be aware of them.

KEY QUESTION

Are we capable of building a genuine, thriving, multi-racial society regardless of history or the colour of a person's skin?

Often black people's reaction to racism has been to close in on themselves, to refuse to be 'absorbed' into the community. Instead, as a means of survival, they may develop their own black social life. They have learned to take pride in their blackness. An example is the religion of Rastafarianism, which originated in the Jamaican slums. Rastafarians believe in the divinity of Haile Selassie, later Emperor of Ethiopia, who they believe was a reincarnation of Jesus. He was seen to be the 'King of Kings', 'Lion of Judah' and 'Root of David' (Revelation 5:5). At the heart of their belief is the rejection of white dominance and the hope of an eventual return to Africa from the evils of the west (Babylon). Rastafarianism has attracted young British blacks of West Indian origin because the divinity of a black man provided a system of belief that was different from the white dominance of traditional Christianity. The life style, and especially the music of the Rastafarians ('reggae'), heavily influenced by the late Bob Marley, helped to formulate this religion of protest against the values of white capitalism and Christianity.

The Caribbean and West African Christian Churches also play an important part in providing their communities with a sense of identity. Whether these churches are attached to mainstream UK denominations or to separate black denominations, the Christian message is seen to offer security against discrimination, especially in its teachings about equality and forgiveness.

Only about 60 out of 11 000 Church of England clergy are black, although the number is growing. There are now at least 750 congregations belonging

REFLECTIONS

'Don't tell me that there is no racism in this so-called tolerant Christian country of yours. We've had National Front slogans daubed on our walls and human excreta shoved down our letter-box. My brother was attacked by three skinheads and put in hospital. Our neighbours have been victims of fire bomb attacks. The police have done nothing, they treat us as second-class citizens. We live in fear.'
(17-year-old Asian girl)

'Young people from ethnic minorities fear the police. They do not respect them. Their fear springs from experience; they are often stopped in the streets to be

questioned and searched; many are racially abused; some are beaten in police custody; and others are criminalized on the perjured evidence of policemen. Parents have come to realize that a Christian upbringing does not safeguard their children from such practices. This is not the judgement of blinkered political extremism; it is the sad and bitter witness of Church members from multi-racial inner city communities throughout the country.'
(*The Church of England and Racism – And Beyond*, Church of England Board for Social Responsibility 1982)

to black clergy and officials. Some of their leaders believe that black churches should develop their own 'theology of protest' clearly expressed in Black Theology (see unit 64) which stresses that 'our dignity as human beings is no longer at the mercy of the image of blacks in the white mind.'

The growth of the black-led churches in Britain is seen by many as being the result of the way the white churches have neglected racism and the black community in the past.

However, the overall Christian message has always been clear. People from all races are the same because they are made in the image of God and are God's children.

> *'Racism is an assault on Christ's values,'*
> (World Council of Churches)

REFLECTIONS

'The leadership of the Church is what I call "politely racist". It does not exercise vulgarity but it is extremely racist. Because of that, they are not able to listen to the black presence in their midst.'
(Reverend Tony Ottey)

'With some dramatic exceptions the British churches took up no positions on race and racism until the late 1960s.'

(Reverend Kenneth Slack)

FOR YOUR FOLDERS

▶ What problems do black people face in Britain?
▶ 'Britain is not without racism.' What examples in this unit bear this statement out? Have you encountered people with racist attitudes in your life?
▶ Explain the beliefs and importance of Rastafarianism.
▶ Why do black groups sometimes 'close in on themselves'?
▶ *'White Christians have often neglected their black brethren.'* Comment.

The growth of the black-led churches in Britain is seen by many as being the result of the way the white churches have in the past ignored the problems caused by racism

KEY WORD

Apartheid – 'Literally apartheid means the keeping separate of races of different colours in one country, especially of Europeans and non-Europeans in South Africa. It is a system whereby a minority regime elected by one small section of the population governs in the interest of, and for the benefit of, the white community.'
(Catholic Institute for International Relations)

The white population of South Africa, numbering about 5 million people, rule over and control the 28 million black people. While the whites enjoy one of the highest standards of living in the world, the great majority of blacks live in poverty and squalor, and have no democratic rights. In 1912 the African National Congress (ANC) was formed and has since been in the forefront of opposition to apartheid. The 1950s witnessed mass resistance by black people but in 1960 the army shot dead 69 protestors at Sharpeville. The ANC was banned and many of its leaders thrown into prison. The South African apartheid regime has brutally crushed any opposition with death sentences, detention, torture, massive censorship of the press and imprisonment.

Many Church leaders, both white and black, have been in the forefront of the opposition to apartheid. The situation in South Africa was most forcibly described to the world in the 1950s by a young Church of England monk called Trevor Huddleston. Huddleston went to South Africa in 1943 and on his return to England in 1956 he published *Nought for Your Comfort*, a powerful attack on apartheid and an account of the black people's struggle for freedom. The book caused much controversy because he criticized the Church for failing to take more of a stand against apartheid.

'Why, if the person is of infinite dignity in the sight of God, does the Church accept so complacently the constant invasions upon personal liberty which occur in South Africa? I do not mean by the "Church", simply the hierarchy, the archbishops and bishops, . . . I mean the Church in its Pauline sense which has "many members", the whole family of God.'
(Trevor Huddleston, *Nought for Your Comfort*, William Collins Sons & Co 1956/1987)

The Church sleeps on. White Christianity is more concerned to retain its character as a law-abiding force than to express its abhorrence of apartheid. In spite of resolutions and announcements the Church as a whole does not care. 'If one member suffers, all the members suffer with it', said St Paul.

'The truth is that the overwhelming majority of white South Africans have no conception whatever of human relationships except that based on racial domination. That there is no time to lose in breaking the present government I am convinced. If this is disloyalty, then I am disloyal. I prefer to believe that Christians are called to a higher obedience.'
(Trevor Huddleston, *Nought for Your Comfort*)

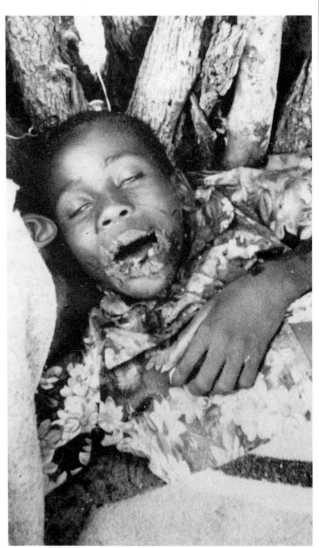

'The child and many others are victims not of the isolated acts of sick individuals but of a concerted attempt by the apartheid regime to repress a new generation, the very future of South Africa' (African National Congress)

Although Trevor Huddleston's book first came out in 1956 it was published again in 1984 and in the preface he wrote:

'It still remains true that no black African has citizenship rights in the 87% of the country declared to belong to white South Africa. Some three and a half million black Africans have been uprooted from their homes without choice and dumped without hope. This is the meaning of apartheid and apartheid is more deeply entrenched than when I wrote this book. Unfortunately the West has largely accepted South Africa's policies and there is, therefore, the danger that South Africa will do what it likes, both inside the country and outside. In this sense South Africa is undoubtedly a threat to world peace.'

Today Trevor Huddleston still tirelessly fights for the liberation of South Africa and is president of the Anti-Apartheid Movement. He believes that the West has a moral duty to put pressure on the South African government, by imposing economic 'sanctions' (not doing business with South Africa): people refusing to buy South African goods and ordinary people becoming involved in campaigning for an end to **apartheid**. Despite growing oppression in South Africa many nations, particularly Britain and the USA continue to do business with the white apartheid regime because of huge investments in South Africa.

Another churchman who consistently speaks out against apartheid is Desmond Tutu, the Archbishop of Capetown. He and many other black Christians have developed 'Black Theology'. Here he describes what Black Theology is:

'Black Theology arises in a context of Black suffering at the hands of rampant white racism. It burns to awaken the White man to the degradation into which he has fallen by de-humanizing the Black man, and so is concerned with the liberation of the oppressor equally as with that of the oppressed. Black Theology has occurred mainly in South Africa, where blacks have had their noses rubbed in the dust by white racism, depersonalizing them to the extent that they have – blasphemy of blasphemies – come to doubt the reality of their own personhood and humanity. Black Theology becomes part of their struggle for liberation; tries to help victims of oppression to assert their humanity and to look at the other chap in the eye and speak face to face without shuffling their feet and apologizing for their Black existence.'

(Archbishop Desmond Tutu, *Hope and Suffering*, William Collins Sons & Co 1984)

TALKING POINT

- 'I hear the words of a song in Crossroads, South Africa, ringing out in my soul today. Those children in the pits of exploitation – no bathrooms, no running water, no right to vote, no political protection – nothing but their religion. They said that just because we are in the slums, the slums are not in us. We will rise above our circumstances.'

   (Reverend Jesse Jackson)

FOR YOUR FOLDERS

- ► Write an article of about 100 words called 'Apartheid today'.
- ► Why was Trevor Huddleston's book controversial?
- ► What does he believe the West should do to rid the world of apartheid?
- ► Explain what Black Theology is.

FOR DISCUSSION

- ► 'The untenable claim of a minority in South Africa is steadily building a wall of intense hate which will result in the most violent and regrettable consequences in the future unless the minority abandons the iniquitous racial policy which it pursues.'

   (Kwame Nkrumah)

65 THE KAIROS DOCUMENT

In 1985, as the situation in South Africa worsened, some South African theologians met in the townships to discuss what the Christian response to the situation should be. They produced the 'Kairos Document' which aroused much controversy among Christians and non-Christians. The word 'kairos' is the Greek word in the Bible meaning 'moment of truth'. One hundred and fifty-one South African theologians signed the document which is inspired by Black Theology. The document offered an analysis of how and why the Church should take action, become involved in civil disobedience, take the side of the oppressed and confront the state in order to obey God. The document raises many important questions about the role of the Church when it finds itself in a crisis situation, particularly in South Africa where basic human rights are being violated every day by a government that claims to be Christian and even uses the Bible to justify its actions. The Kairos Document reflects the views of many ordinary Christians in South Africa, who live in the shanty towns and townships, and it reflects the anger and frustration that they feel.

In this reflection we shall look at some extracts of the document which, although not final, is part of the ongoing debate about the Christian response to the explosive and dangerous situation in Southern Africa.

REFLECTION

'The moment of truth has arrived. The Church is divided. We sit in the same Church while outside Christian policemen and soldiers are beating up and killing Christian children or torturing Christian prisoners to death while yet other Christians stand by and weakly plead for peace.

The South African state has a theology of its own. Throughout the history of Christianity totalitarian regimes have tried to legitimize an attitude of blind obedience and servility towards the state by using the Bible ("Every person must submit to the supreme authorities." (Romans 13:1)). But in the rest of the Bible God does not demand obedience to oppressive rulers. This state theology believes that the government has the God-given right to use violence to enforce its system of law and order. The State's effort to preserve law and order, which should imply the protection of human life, means the very opposite for the majority of the people, namely the suppression and destruction of life. The State in its oppression of the people makes use again and again of the name of God. Their god is an idol, a god who is historically on the side of the white settlers, who dispossesses black people of their land and who gives most of the land to "his chosen people". It is tne god of superior weapons who conquered those who were armed with nothing but spears. It is the god of teargas, rubber bullets, prison cells and death sentences. The government uses Christianity to justify its evil ways and there are churches like the white Dutch Reformed Churches who actually subscribe to this blasphemy.

Church Theology uses the idea of

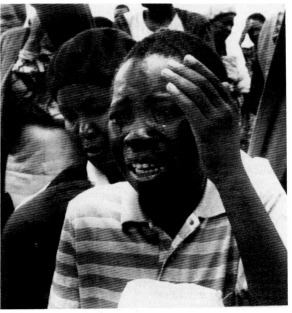

'We sit in the same church while outside Christian policemen and soldiers are beating up and killing Christian children'

"Reconciliation". There can be no true reconciliation and no genuine peace without justice. Reconciliation will become our Christian duty in South Africa only when the apartheid regime shows signs of genuine repentance. The continued military repression of the people in the townships and the jailing of its opponents is clear proof of the total lack of repentance on behalf of the apartheid regime. The problem we are dealing with in South Africa is "structural violence and injustice". People are *suffering, people are being maimed, killed, tortured every day. We can't sit back and wait for the oppressor to see the light so that the oppressed can put out their hands and beg for the crumbs of some small reforms. True justice, God's justice demands a radical change of structures. God does not bring his justice through a few reforms introduced by the Pharoahs of this world.*

Church Theology professes non-violence. But many church leaders support the growing militarization of South Africa. How can one condemn violence and then appoint chaplains to a very violent army? Is it because the activities of the armed forces and police are counted as defensive? Why are the activities of young blacks in the townships not regarded as defensive? The problem of the Church here is that it starts from the idea that the apartheid regime is a legitimate authority. It ignores the fact that it is a white minority regime which has imposed itself upon the majority of the people, that is blacks, in this country and that it maintains itself by brutality and violent force and the fact that a majority of South Africans regard this regime as illegitimate. In practice what one calls "violence" and what one calls "self-defence" seems to depend upon which side one is on.

Prophetic theology

Prophecy is always confrontational. It condemns the evil of the times and speaks out against it in no uncertain terms. Prophecy must name the sins of apartheid as "an offence against God". Prophecy must announce the hopeful news of liberation, justice and peace, naming the ways of bringing this about and encouraging people to take action. The people of Israel were oppressed internally ("We are being massacred daily." (Psalm 44:22)). The oppressors benefit and accumulate great wealth. Millions benefit in no way. They are treated as labour units, paid starvation wages, separated from their families, moved about like cattle and dumped in homelands to starve – all for the benefit of a privileged minority. They are no longer prepared to be crushed and are determined to change this system even at the cost of their own lives. A regime that has made itself the enemy of the people has made itself the enemy of God.

The Church of Jesus Christ is not called to be a bastion of caution and moderation. We must participate in the cross of Christ if we are to have hope of participating in his resurrection. The Church should inspire us to make sacrifices for justice and liberation. The Church must preach this message not only in words but also through its actions.'

(The Kairos Document, Catholic Institute for International Relations, 1985)

FOR YOUR FOLDERS

After reading this reflection answer the following questions:

- ► *'The moment of truth has arrived'.* Comment on this statement.
- ► How does the document attack 'Church Theology'?
- ► Why does the document rule out the idea of reconciliation at the present time?
- ► What is 'structural violence'?
- ► Explain what the document means by 'prophetic theology'.

TALKING POINT

- • **'The state in its oppression of the people makes use again and again of the name of God. Their god is an idol who is historically on the side of the white settlers, and who dispossesses black people; it is the god of superior weapons, the god of tear gas, rubber bullets, prison cells and death sentences.'**

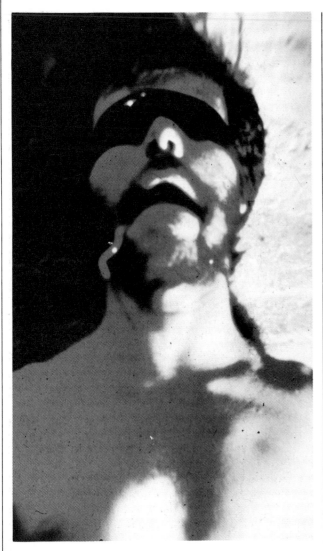

Almost half the countries in the world have governments which practise torture

As human beings we all have certain rights. The right to life, freedom, liberty, work, health care, housing, education. In 1948 these and many other rights were enshrined in the Universal Declaration of Human Rights which was signed by governments of countries all over the world.

However we live in a world in which millions of people every day have their rights denied or violated. This section is concerned with one of the most vicious violations of human rights, namely torture.

Although torture is illegal under international law it is practised by over half of the governments of the world. Torture is a crime against humanity. It is cruel and barbaric. The methods of torture vary but the aim of the torturers is the same – to inflict the greatest possible amount of pain on the victim. The results are the same – broken bodies and minds. Torture degrades the torturer as well as the victim. Most of us, thankfully, can only begin to imagine what a terrifying thing it is to be tortured. It can only be described as a living hell, yet while you read this hundreds of people in the world are being tortured now.

One Christian organization that is concerned with torture is ACT (Action by Christians against torture).

act: What is it?

Action by Christians against Torture is a campaign sponsored by the British Council of Churches.

ACT's aim is "to increase awareness in the churches, both nationally and locally, of the need, for reasons of Christian faith, to campaign against torture and to work for its abolition wherever and on whoever it is used."

act: Why?

"This Assembly, in obedience to the biblical teaching on the dignity of human life and in keeping with existing human rights agreements, declares that the use of torture by any Government, group or individual in any place, at any time, for any reason, is to be condemned."

British Council of Churches Assembly, 1981

Torture is a crime against God and humanity. **ACT** offers an opportunity for churches to campaign ecumenically against this evil and to support the victims of human rights abuse.

Because our faith sets at its centre a symbol of torture: the cross. So we should be especially sensitive about torture and strive to make the resurrection promise a reality in people's lives by working to resist this intolerable evil.

Because we understand God to be the source of life, the upholder of justice, the origin of goodness. So we should affirm the things of life, and fight against all those of death – which includes torture.

(Action by Christians Against Torture)

THINGS TO DO

▶ Write to ACT and Amnesty International (see address section) to find out more about their work.

REFLECTION

Buras Nhlabathi interrogated and tortured for three months in South Africa.

'On 8 October 1986 I was arrested at 3.30 am. I was taken from the house I was staying at by force and beaten with fists, kicked and hit with the butt of guns. This went on for about 45 minutes.

I was then thrown into the back of a van with twelve comrades arrested at the same time. We were taken to Kenbasi police station and initially left outside in the rain. I was taken into an interrogation room and questioned about posters and leaflets of banned organizations. When I refused to answer I was beaten. This went on for about 5 hours; they hit me with keys and pipes and sjamboks. I had no sleep and they kept me on my feet.

I was also given electric shocks from handcuffs. I did not answer the questions, preferring to die.

On the second day I was stripped and put into a rubber suit from head to foot. A dummy was placed in my mouth so I couldn't scream. There was no air. They switched the plug on. My muscles were pumping hard. I couldn't see anything. When they switched the plug off they took the dummy out and said I should speak. When I refused they put the dummy back and switched on again.

After a long time they switched off. I was stripped and put into a fridge naked. I was left there. I was then brought out again and put into the electric shock suit.

Then I was taken into an interrogation room. My hands and feet and my head were tied to a pole and bright search lights turned on. I felt my mind go dead. I couldn't see. I was dizzy. I was beaten again. I have scars on my right hip.

I was then taken to Madupo prison. I was given ice cubes for my face but no medical treatment. I was in prison for three months. I spent two weeks in solitary confinement. I was beaten in prison, just slapped. I was not charged or tried or convicted of any offence.

After my release I was to report at 7.00 am and 7.00 pm every day. I didn't. I spent five months in hiding before my escape.'
Buras now lives in exile.

(Anti-Apartheid News)

A TESTIMONY

I have experienced the fate of a victim. I have seen the torturer's face at close quarters. It was in a worse condition than my own bleeding, livid face. The torturer's was distorted by a kind of twitching that had nothing human about it. He was in such a state of tension that he had an expression very similar to those we see on Chinese masks; I am not exaggerating. It is not an easy thing to torture people. It requires inner participation. In this situation, I turned out to be the lucky one. I was humiliated. I did not humiliate others. I was simply bearing a profoundly unhappy humanity in my aching entrails. Whereas the men who humiliate you must first humiliate the notion of humanity within themselves. Never mind if they strut around in uniforms, swollen with the knowledge that they can control the suffering, sleeplessness, hunger and despair of their fellow human beings, intoxicated with the power in their hands. Their intoxication is nothing other than the degradation of humanity. The ultimate degradation. They have had to pay dearly for my torments. I wasn't the one in the worst position. I was simply a man who moaned because he was in great pain. I prefer that. At this moment I am deprived of the joy of seeing children going to school or playing in the park. Whereas they have to look their own children in the face.

Geo Mangakis 'Letter to Europeans', *Index*, Vol No 1 (reprinted in 'Amnesty International report on torture')

FOR YOUR FOLDERS

▶ In 'A Testimony', who suffers the 'ultimate degradation' according to Geo Mangakis?
▶ After reading the account of torture in South Africa write a letter to the South African government expressing your view.
▶ Why do Christians see torture as a crime against humanity and God?
▶ Explain in your own words the aims of ACT.

The world music phenomenon is bringing people from all backgrounds and cultures together

REFLECTION

'Music has always been important to me, but I was never so passionate about it until a few years ago when I heard African music for the first time. Now every day is a new adventure; coming across totally different sounds and listening to different cultures' influence upon each other. I listen to the radio and used to watch programmes like 'Top of the Pops' – I see that the popular music of Britain today is lacking in direction and devoid of spirit. However, I do see hope for the western music scene with popular artists like Sting and Bruce Springstein starting to create music with artists from different parts of the world. Around the world music is used as a very important medium for informing people about the realities of life – singing about, for example, our God, our environment or human rights. It's not necessary to understand the words; the harmonies and rhythms of African music, for example, touch parts of ourselves far deeper than mere words will ever be able to.

Music is so basic to our roots and everyone can enjoy it – people of all ages, all races, no matter what their religion is. The 'World Music phenomenon' is bringing people together – people from the country and people from the cities. Through music we can find a more joyous way of living. We can increase our understanding of other cultures and we can increase our understanding about ourselves and our relationship with God. No matter where we live in the world we are all cells of God – if only we could realize it and join together.

I was brought up in Roman Catholic schools but, despite this, when I was younger I had little understanding of what God meant. It was just a word. Now when I listen to the harmonies of the Black South African Christians, or the griots of Mali or the Sufi praise singers from Pakistan, I understand that their God is the same as ours. It seems so simple yet wars are being fought over religions. I see music as the most powerful and most immediate way by which we can come together, unite and see that actually there is only one world, not three.'

(Steve Turner, World Music DJ and promoter)

For Christians and followers of all religious traditions, the arts are a powerful way of expressing beliefs and ideas. Throughout the ages Christian ideas have been expressed through art, literature and music. Of all the arts, the one most celebrated and nourished in the Christian West has been music. For centuries music has been enormously influenced by Christian ideas – from the hymns of the early Church, through the works of the great classical composers to popular music in the twentieth century.

In this section we are looking at a modern musical phenomenon that is beginning to change the way that people look at the world in which they live – World Music.

THINGS TO DO

▶ Explain why you think this logo was designed to represent World Music?

THINKING POINTS

- 'If rock is the first universal language, and I believe it is, and the majority of the world's population is under twenty five then you can shape and mould and direct their intentions positively with music. Music itself doesn't change the world, people change the world; but music can be a powerful instrument of information.'
  (Peter Gabriel)
- 'There is no charm in the whole realm of art so subtle, so intangible as that of music. It is the most spiritual of all modes of expression.'
  (William Temple, Archbishop of Canterbury 1942–1944)

FOR DISCUSSION

▶ 'Music is about changing the mind, not to understand but to be more aware.' (John Cage)

FOR YOUR FOLDERS

▶ After reading this section explain what you think Peter Gabriel means when he says, 'music can be a powerful instrument of information'. Give examples.
▶ In what ways has World Music changed Steve Turner's ideas about God and the world?

Through music we can find a more joyous way of living

Millions of people around the world live in inadequate housing

Not just statistics

1 More is spent on armaments in one day than the world's two billion poorest people have to live on in one year.
2 More people have died as a consequence of hunger in the past six years than have been killed in all wars, revolutions and murders in the past 150 years.
3 35 000 people die every day as a result of hunger.

These are not just statistics. Nor are the hungry faces we often see on our television screens just images. They are people, human beings, like us. Millions upon millions of people like us suffer the torments of poverty every day of their lives. They are people with dreams and fears; people who love and are loved; people who, like us, hope for a future filled with joy. Cruelly, because of the arms trade, big business interests, superpower struggles, racism, injustice, exploitation, ignorance and complacency, many of these people have no hope for the future at all.

The Bible and poverty

In the Old Testament much reference is made to God's concern for the victims of poverty, injustice and oppression and great stress is put on helping these people. Again in the New Testament Jesus is involved and concerned for the poor in society. Jesus teaches that those with material wealth should give it to the poor.

> *'If you wish to go the whole way, go, sell your possessions and give to the poor, then you will have treasures in heaven . . . I tell you this: a rich man will find it hard to enter the Kingdom of heaven. I repeat it is easier for a camel to pass through the eye of a needle than for a rich man to enter the Kingdom of God.'*
> (Matthew 19:22, 24)

TALKING POINTS

- 'As long as there is poverty in the world I can never be rich, even if I have a million dollars. I can never be what I ought to be until you are what you ought to be.'
  (Martin Luther King)

- 'A Church that is in solidarity with the poor can never be a wealthy Church. It must sell all in a sense to follow its Master. It must use its wealth and resources for the sake of the least of Christ's brethren.'
  (Archbishop Desmond Tutu)

Some Christian organizations

CHRISTIAN AID

Christian Aid raises money to help the neediest people in poor countries to help themselves. In times of war and disaster it tries to give relief and rehabilitation. In Britain it tries to make people aware of world poverty and its causes. Nearly half of its income comes from the annual Christian Aid week each May. Out of every £1 donated, 85p is spent on aid projects. Only 15p is needed for fund raising, advertising, staff, offices, etc. In areas of poverty Christian Aid finances agricultural training, equipment, livestock, seeds and irrigation, trade training, child welfare, instruction in nutrition and hygiene, community health schemes, education in community development and legal aid when people's human rights are threatened. In areas of emergency it finances medical supplies, food and blankets, transport and building materials, all for use by local relief agencies. Refugees are sheltered, fed and helped to resettle.

CAFOD (CATHOLIC FUND FOR OVERSEAS DEVELOPMENT)

CAFOD is another agency that tries to help the needy of the world. For instance, in South Africa, CAFOD provides money to help the Church there to give emergency assistance to victims of the apartheid system.

CAAT (CAMPAIGN AGAINST THE ARMS TRADE)

CAAT works to make people aware of the evil of the arms trade – a major cause of poverty and misery.

TEAR FUND

Money raised by the Tear Fund is used for both emergency relief and long-term development. It funds Christian volunteers who work on medical, agricultural, educational and community development projects.

THINGS TO DO

▶ None of us is powerless. Begin by writing to an organization concerned with world poverty (see *Some important addresses*, p. 156) and request more information. If you want to, you could give up sweets, crisps, etc. for just a few days and send a donation, as every penny helps somebody. Remember, we are not talking just about statistics.

FOR YOUR FOLDERS

▶ The Church has enormous wealth worldwide. Do you think it could do more to help the world's poor? If so, what?

▶ Look up the following references in the Bible: Deuteronomy 24:19; Luke 3:11; John 3:17–18. Write the passages down. How are they related to world poverty? What Christian beliefs do you think inspire many Christians to work for the world's poor?

! ▶ *'If Christ's teaching, 'Go, sell your possessions, and give to the poor', was followed by the world's Christians, then we would have a wonderful, gentle, revolution on our hands.'* Comment.

69 CHRISTIANS OF THE REVOLUTION – LIBERATION THEOLOGY

'People are always worried about the violence done with machine guns and machetes. But there is another kind of violence that you must be aware of too. To watch your children die of sickness and hunger while you can do nothing is a violence of the spirit. We have suffered silently for too many years.'

(El Salvadorean peasant)

Latin America is a continent rich in natural resources. However, the vast majority of its people are trapped in poverty and squalor. Many of the countries are ruled by a wealthy and powerful elite. For instance, in El Salvador 60 per cent of the land is owned by fourteen powerful families. Millions of people suffer not only from poverty but also from oppression by governments. The few people in power are prepared to keep their power at all costs. Torture, assassinations and 'death squads' are the harsh realities if anyone dares oppose these governments.

'In its zeal to get rid of the guerillas the Argentinian military unleashed a whirlwind which developed its own horrific momentum. Intellectuals, trade unionists, teachers, students and journalists were rounded up and taken to one of the three hundred and forty secret detention centres dotted around the country. Most were tortured, murdered, then buried in rubbish dumps and secret graveyards. Then the friends and acquaintances of the victims were taken away. Most of the children who disappeared were parcelled out for adoption, though some were almost certainly murdered. 30 000 Argentinians disappeared, the vast majority completely innocent of any crime'.

(*New Internationalist*, January 1988)

In 1968 a conference of bishops met in Medellin in Colombia. Concerned with the general situation in Latin America, they declared:

'In many places in Latin America there is a situation of injustice that must be recognized as insitutionalized violence, because the existing structures violate people's basic rights; a situation which calls for far-reaching, daring and urgent action.'

The bishops recognized the temptation to resort to revolutionary violence to change the system, and recognized that in some cases such action is justifiable. But they also warned that such violence would not really improve things in the long term. They stressed the need for the people to be given 'liberation'. The term 'Liberation Theology' became popular. Many priests have become active in joining movements to fight injustice and oppression and many more are prepared to speak out. A Colombian Roman Catholic priest, Camilo Torres, summed up Liberation Theology when he said:

'Revolution is necessary to free the hungry, give drink to the thirsty, clothe the naked and procure a life of well-being for the needy majority. I believe that the revolutionary struggle is appropriate for the Christian. Only by revolution, by changing the concrete conditions of our country, can we enable men to practise love for each other.'

(John Geriffi (ed.), *CAMILO TORRES, Revolutionary Priest*, Penguin 1973)

Torres himself, realizing that the Colombian government would violently crush any peaceful resistance, joined a guerilla movement. In 1966 he was killed by government troops in a skirmish.

Gustavo Gutierrez, a leading Liberation Theology thinker, wrote of the Church's role in the past:

'The Church has devoted her attention to formulating truths and meanwhile did almost nothing to better the world. This must now cease.'

(Gustavo Gutierrez)

He also quotes the New Testament to show that Jesus' message was one of liberation:

'As much as you have done this (fed the hungry, clothed the naked, visited the sick and the prisoners) *to the least of my bretheren you have done it to me.'*

(Matthew 25:40)

'But alas for you who are rich; you have had your time of happiness.
Alas for you who are well-fed now; you shall go hungry.'

(Luke 6:24, 25)

TALKING POINTS

- 'The Catholic who is not a revolutionary is living in mortal sin.'

  (Camilo Torres)
- 'When I give food to the poor they call me a saint. When I ask why the poor have no food, they call me a Communist.'

  (Helder Camera)

Father Ted

It started in the slums of Brazil. Now 'liberation theology' reaches from Sao Paulo to Sydney. James Murray talks to Ted Kennedy, an outspoken Australian priest with a passion for the poor.

Caught between the new immigrants are the original inhabitants of Australia – its aboriginal people. Disinherited by European settlement they've turned from being free-ranging hunters to being the poorest of Australia's citizens.

Ted Kennedy has been a familiar Redfern resident for years. A nervy and pugnacious Catholic priest, the local aboriginal people call him Father Ted. He is a maverick and he knows it. He is also a bit of a loner, passionately concerned with the welfare of his aboriginal parishioners but isolated from a complete understanding of their problems by his white skin. Like his fellow priests, he says he has 'never known the perspective that comes from behind the black screen'.

Father Ted has a passion for the Gospel and is thankful to aboriginal friends for opening his eyes to its deeper meanings. His reading of some Biblical passages may surprise the orthodox, but they are the fruit of much reflection. 'I believe in putting real, live people, namely the poor, at the centre of the church's concern,' he says.

His is an Australian brand of the original liberation theology born in the slums of Latin America. And it is a theology which seeks to redefine religious concepts which are tainted by the past. 'Mission' is one of them. 'To many aboriginal people,' he explains, 'it is an ugly, burnt-out word carrying only memories of moral repression and suffering which went under the name of Christian.'

'Missionaries would have us believe their mission comes directly from heaven. But how can they be godsends to people they haven't even met? There's a strong whiff of theological imperialism in the concept of mission,' he says.

'Property' is another concern. he has been instrumental in helping Redfern's aboriginal people gain freehold title to most of the Catholic Church property in the parish. Though he found at one stage that 'the last thing a religious order is ready to face up to is the handing over of property'.

If to some he seems obsessed with the aboriginal people, God seems to have left him no other constituency. 'I think I'm seen as some kind of father,' he muses. 'They find a father figure meaningful.' And he quotes with some force an aboriginal girl's remark. 'I wouldn't want to have anything to do with you whites,' she said, 'unless you knew your liberation was bound up with mine'.

You sense a discreet but palpable affection for him from Redfern's street people. And when he speaks of his own 'mission', he talks about those people he has known and worked with for decades. 'My real aim,' he says, 'is to introduce the rich to the poor, at a very personal level.'

For him, charities which only convince the wealthy to part with their old clothes end up separating the poor from the rich. They don't allow the rich to experience what it is to be poor, or even to observe the effects of poverty. Ted Kennedy sees this as a self-defeating denial, since he believes strongly that it is only through the poor that Christ claims his identity.

'You are automatically stripped,' he declares, 'when you become friends with the poor, and you lose some of your moral security. But the poor have the kingdom in their possession. And it's only via the poor that we can ever hope to gain salvation.'

As he looks out across the gate of the church, a taxi blithely ignores a group of aborigine men wanting a ride to the city. Their shouts follow the driver's rapidly disappearing shape. 'Damn', one of them mutters darkly, 'Us abos always have to stand at the end of the line.'

The parish priest of Redfern, at least, is in the queue with them.

New Internationalist, No 155, Jan. 1986

FOR YOUR FOLDERS

▶ Write a short article called 'Injustice in Latin America'.

▶ Explain in your own words what you understand by the phrase 'Liberation Theology.'

▶ *'Blessed are the peacemakers'* (Matthew 5:9). Do you think that in the light of this teaching Christians are still justified in resorting to revolutionary violence?

▶ *'Every person must submit to the supreme authorities.'* (Romans 13:1). How might Gutierrez or Camilo Torres respond to these words by St Paul?

▶ Write an article of about 100 words on Liberation Theology in Australia.

FOR DISCUSSION

▶ 'For the Aborigines 'mission' is an ugly burnt out word carrying only memories of moral repression and suffering which went under the name of Christian.'

70 CHRISTIANS OF THE REVOLUTION – NICARAGUA

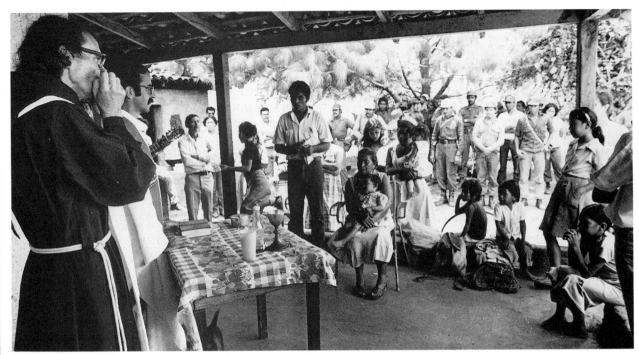

'In Nicaragua a man of God can't turn his back on political struggle'

As you have seen in the last unit, some Roman Catholic priests have felt inspired by their Christian faith to make a stand against injustice. In 1979, in the small central American country of Nicaragua, the people, inspired and supported by many churchmen, took part in a revolution to overthrow a corrupt and unjust government.

Since 1936, Nicaragua had been ruled by one family called the Somozas. The majority of the three million inhabitants of Nicaragua lived in conditions of dreadful poverty. Eighty per cent had no running water; 50 per cent were unemployed; 45 per cent earned less than £50 a year; of every 100 children born, ten died from disease before they were five

REFLECTIONS

'I'd seen the most humiliated, the most miserable, the most oppressed of Nicaragua. I tried to respond in a Christian way, peacefully promoting social and human development, and with the few government resources. But I realized it was all a lie. I was discouraged to see that all the work meant nothing. The people continued living the same. And so I joined the armed struggle knowing that nothing peaceful was possible . . . any other way would have been dishonest to my people and to myself.'
(Father Laviana – died in combat 1978)

'The repression was incredible. The National Guard pulled people out of their houses, put their shirts over their heads – so all we'd see in the backs of their jeeps was this naked kid with his head forced down. . . . people just disappeared and there was nothing we could do . . . except try and change this country in the name of God and for the sake of God.'
(Sister Juliana)

'In Nicaragua a man of God can't turn his back on political struggle. At Mass we discussed the Gospels with the peasants and they began to understand the divine message: the coming of God's kingdom; which is the establishment on earth of a just society. At first we had preferred to make a non-violent . revolution, but later came to understand that right now, in Nicaragua, non-violent struggle is not possible.'
(Father Cardenal)

years old. The Somaza family and its supporters got richer and mercilessly crushed any opposition, by using death squads which took people from their homes, tortured and often killed them.

However, opposition to the government grew, especially within certain sectors of the Church. Many priests and nuns, inspired by Liberation Theology, spoke out against the government. In the reflections we can begin to understand why many Christians decided to take part in an armed uprising to bring about justice in Nicaragua.

In 1979, after a long struggle, the people overthrew the Somoza government. The new government, called the Sandinistas, consisted of many of the priests who had taken part in the revolution. The government began working for justice in Nicaragua. It reduced illiteracy, eradicated polio, built schools and hospitals, reduced infant mortality rates, gave everyone free health care, gave ordinary people power in their communities and much else.

Central America is often called the 'back yard of the USA'. For many years American governments have been worried that socialist-style governments might gain power in Central America, and so they often give help to governments like the Somozas.

Since 1981 the USA has funded the 'contras', supporters of the overthrown Somoza government. The contras attack the farms, schools and hospitals in Nicaragua hoping to overthrow the people's government. The highest court in the world, the International Court of Justice, has declared that the USA-backed war against Nicaragua is illegal and many leading Christians in the USA have spoken out against the continuing war.

FOR YOUR FOLDERS

▶ Write an article called 'Nicaragua – before and after the struggle'.
▶ Explain how Liberation Theology has inspired many Nicaraguan churchmen.
▶ Explain why Fathers Laviana and Cardenal joined the armed struggle.
▶ On a visit to Nicaragua, Pope John Paul II criticized the revolutionary priests. Can you think of some reasons why he might have criticized them?

Revolutionary joy in Nicaragua, 1979

71 WAR AND PEACE

The early Christian Church was strictly pacifist, but once the Emperor Constantine adopted Christianity in 313 CE as the state religion the Church found excuses for not condemning war. Many reasons were advanced over the centuries to explain how it was morally acceptable for Christians to kill human beings whether they be Christians or people of other faiths. By the thirteenth century CE Christianity had adopted the theory of a 'just war'. Basically the theory of the just war maintained that under certain conditions it was acceptable to engage in warfare, for instance if the war helped to restore peace and justice, or if those attacked were attacked because they had committed some grave wrong. Christianity also adopted the theory known as the 'holy war', which basically meant that God was on their side, particularly if the war was thought to protect the faith.

However, in the past these theories have often been abused by both governments and Churches. For instance, in the slaughter of the First World War theologians on both the German and British sides maintained that God was on their side.

Christianity, like all the world's religions, teaches the wisdom of peace, forgiveness, love and trust. Yet Christianity, like other religions, has followers who have interpreted these teachings to suit their own ends. The teachings of Jesus in the Gospels are clear, yet Christians have killed and continue to kill other people who are supposed, like them, to be God's children.

The twentieth century has witnessed some of the most brutal and widespread wars in human history. Wars continue to rage in our world today, destroying human lives and causing untold human misery. Yet we live in a society that uses war as entertainment. Films like *Rambo* fill our cinemas, glorifying the horrors of war. Toy manufacturers continue to produce war toys; publishers produce war magazines; television churns out old war movies; film-makers continue to produce videos full of horror and violence. It is as if young people are being slowly conditioned to accept war as the norm, trained to accept violence. Some people, Christians among them, strongly believe that the increasing violence in our society is a product of these things.

The economic cost of warfare is staggering. The developed countries spend twenty times more on their military programmes than on economic aid to the poor countries of the world where millions face starvation. To keep military expenditure at its present level, every working person will have to sacrifice from three to four years of their income to the arms race. This is one of the major causes of world poverty. In the last two years more people have died from hunger than were killed in both world wars.

Christianity has obviously not done enough to bring the message of peace and goodwill into the hearts and minds of everyone. For some reason many people believe that war is inevitable and part of human nature, but it does not have to be like this. Here are some 'Thoughts for your future'.

THOUGHTS FOR YOUR FUTURE

'World peace is not only possible but inevitable. It is the next stage in the evolution of this planet. For the first time in history we can view the entire planet. It is time for the planetization of humankind, the unification of all the peoples of the world in one universal family. Humanity stands today at the crossroads. The path of the future remains open, subject to a choice which has yet to be made. One road leads to peace, the other to self-destruction.'
(Javier Perez de Cuellar, Secretary General of the United Nations)

'Our future on this planet depends on one single factor; humanity must make a moral about-face.'
(Pope John Paul II)

'Violence is the way of barbarians, non-violence is the way of men.'
(Mahatma Gandhi)

'They shall beat their swords into mattocks and their spears into pruning-knives; nations shall not lift sword against nation nor ever again be trained for war.'
(Micah 4:3)

'Put up your sword. All who take the sword die by the sword.'
(Matthew 26:52)

Pacifism

*'I believe that all war and violence is wrong. They are
acts against God's will. We are all God's children; we
all have a right to live. Violence only breeds violence.
Nothing good can come out of something evil. We have
been fighting for too long. Untold millions have died at
the hands of others. Now is the time to stop. There is a
better way. Pacifism has never been tried. We must
resist violence. We can explore outer space. Let us now
explore inner space and reject that most base thing – to
hit out blindly. We can do it. It takes far more courage
to resist violence than to engage in it. The world is
crying out for us – for you – to take our destiny in our
hands and bring peace into this beautiful world of
ours.'*

(A pacifist, author's interview)

A Christian pacifist protesting against the arms trade

FOR DISCUSSION

▶ 'Hatred and bitterness can never cure
the disease of fear, only love can do that.
Hatred paralyses life; love releases it.
Hatred confuses life; love harmonizes it.
Hatred darkens life; love illumines it.'

(Martin Luther King)

FOR YOUR FOLDERS

▶ Explain the theories of a just war and a
holy war. How do you think Christians
have justified these theories in the light of
Jesus' teachings about forgiveness and
love?

! ▶ *'People make money out of war and
violence and pollute the minds of the
young.'* Comment.

! ▶ Design a poster with the theme 'Peace'
using some of the ideas in 'Thoughts for
your future'.

! ▶ How do you think the Church can help to
bring about peace on earth?

TALKING POINTS

● 'An eye for an eye and the world will
soon be blind.'

(Mahatma Gandhi)

● 'We are now faced with the fact that
tomorrow is today. We are confronted
with the fierce urgency of NOW. Over
the bleached bones of numerous
civilizations are written the pathetic
words "too late". We still have a choice
today; non-voilent coexistence or violent
coannihilation. This may well be our last
chance to choose between chaos and
community.'

(Martin Luther King)

Everyone on earth lives under the threat of nuclear war. Most of us try to avoid thinking about it. But it is reality. Many young people believe that 'Armageddon', the end of the world, will happen in their lifetimes, either deliberately or by mistake. In Britain there are nuclear bases and nuclear missiles, and the military and the government are ready, if need be, to wage nuclear war. These weapons of mass destruction are all around us, hidden and waiting. We have the power to destroy life on earth. Perhaps if we thought about it we'd go mad. Perhaps by not thinking about it Armageddon draws closer? In this unit are some 'Thinking points' to help you discuss and debate nuclear weapons, their implications and the responses of some Christians.

THINKING POINTS

- 'What is required of us is neither very much nor very difficult. All it would take now to get out of danger would be to raise our "nuclear consciousness". And everyone from the Mexican street peddler to the Manhattan bureaucrat or to the Marseilles fishmonger can do something about that without so much as lifting a finger. The bomb is saying the same thing to everybody.'

   (Derrick de Kerckhove)

- Only a minute after a one megaton groundburst hydrogen bomb hit the Town Hall, very little of Leeds would remain standing. Immediately on detonation there would be a blinding flash of light and deadly nuclear radiation would be emitted. Within three seconds an intensely hot fireball some 9000 feet across would be formed. The familiar mushroom shaped cloud would then rise into the sky. A blastwave travelling faster than the speed of sound and winds of up to 200 miles an hour would spread across the city.'

   (*Leeds and the Bomb*, Leeds City Council 1983)

- 'I think the prophecies are quite clear, that there is the possibility of one-quarter of the human race being destroyed at some point in history under the judgement of God, and God may allow man to have his atomic war, but in the midst of it, before man has destroyed himself, because that would be Armageddon, then God is going to intervene, Christ will set up His kingdom, and to me that is a glorious hope.'

   (Billy Graham – American evangelist)

- 'The acceptance of God's will preached by all religions means there's nothing we can do about it and we don't need to trouble ourselves with it – an excellent cop-out and denial of responsibility, but I suppose it helps the wretched starving millions whose children die in infancy to survive and bear their dreadful lives. It also stops them blaming greedy governments for their plight; all very handy for governments.'
(Margaret Ballard in Dorothy Rowe, *Living with the Bomb*, Routledge and Kegan Paul 1985)

- 'German Christians have destroyed French Christians, English Christians have obliterated German and Italian Christians. Over the centuries, European Christians have slaughtered their brothers and sisters in Christ by the millions.

   Now we have plans to do it by tens of millions. A higher percentage of the total population attends church in the Soviet Union each Sunday than in Western Europe. Atheistic communism has not been able to halt the expansion of Christianity in the Soviet Union. If Christianity perishes there it will not be due to atheistic communism. It will happen because European and American Christians approved of a nuclear policy that culminated in a holocaust destroying 70 million Soviet Christians.

   Do we not crucify Christ anew when we kill other members of his body?'
(Ronald Sider and Richard Taylor – American evangelical theologians, *Nuclear Holocaust and Christian Hope*, Hodder and Stoughton 1982)

- 'Each of us structures and creates our own world. Because we are free to create our world and ourselves we are free to change our world and ouselves. We can choose to see ourselves as capable of change, and, doing so, the future opens up before us in an infinite array of possibilities. Or we can choose to see ourselves as unable to change, forced to live our lives as we have always lived them. Making this choice we are thus doomed to repeat our errors until the culmination of our errors brings the extinction of a species more intelligent but less wise and adaptable than the dinosaurs. Oh, the sorrow and the pity of it all. Choosing not to change means choosing death. Choosing to change means choosing life.'

  (Dorothy Rowe – psychologist, *Living with the Bomb*, Routledge and Kegan Paul 1985)

- 'To remember the past is to commit oneself to the future. To remember Hiroshima is to commit oneself to peace. To remember what the people of this city suffered is to renew our faith in man, in his capacity to do what is good, in his freedom to do what is right, in his determination to turn disaster into a new beginning. Humanity is not destined to self-destruction. Clashes of ideologies, aspirations and needs can and must be settled, and resolved by means other than war and violence.'

  (Pope John Paul II, at the Peace Memorial in Hiroshima)

- 'How can I love people while I threaten to burn them and turn their cities into ashes?'

  (Bruce Kent, Roman Catholic and leading campaigner of CND)

The Pope visits a victim of Hiroshima (1981) – 'To remember Hiroshima is to commit oneself to peace'

73 THIS SACRED PLANET

In the past, European colonization and exploitation of the world, heavily influenced by Christianity (see unit 13) have led to the widespread environmental problems that we as human beings are slowly becoming aware of. In this section are two different reflections about 'this sacred planet'.

REFLECTIONS

'The Great Chief in Washington sends word that he wishes to buy our land. The Great Chief also sends us words of friendship and good will. This is kind of him, since we know he has little need of our friendship in return. But we will consider your offer. For we know that if we do not sell, the white man may come with guns and take our land.

How can you buy or sell the sky, the warmth of the land? The idea is strange to us. If we do not own the freshness of the air and the sparkle of the water, how can you buy them?

Every part of this earth is sacred to my people. Every shining pine needle, every sandy shore, every mist in the dark woods, every clearing and humming insect is holy in the memory and experience of my people. The sap which courses through the trees carries the memories of the red man . . . this land is sacred to us.

This shining water that moves in the streams and rivers is not just water but the blood of our ancestors. If we sell you land, you must remember that it is sacred, and you must teach your children that it is sacred, and that each ghostly reflection in the clear water of the lakes tells of events and memories in the life of my people. The water's murmur is the voice of my father's father.

I do not know. Our ways are different from your ways. The sight of your cities pains the eyes of the red man. But perhaps it is because the red man is a savage and does not understand.

There is no quiet place in the white man's cities. No place to hear the unfurling of leaves in spring or the rustle of insects' wings. But perhaps it is because I am a savage and do not understand. The clatter only seems to insult the ears. And what is there to life if a man cannot hear the lonely cry of the whippoorwill or the arguments of the frogs around a pond at night? I am a red man and do not understand. The Indian prefers the soft sound of the wind darting over the face of a pond, the smell of the wind itself, cleansed by a midday rain, or scented with the pinon pine.

The air is precious to the red man, for all things

share the same breath – the beast, the tree, the man, they all share the same breath. The white man does not seem to notice the air he breathes. Like a man dying for many days, he is numb to the stench. But if we sell our land, you must keep it apart and sacred as a place where even the white man can go to taste the wind that is sweetened by the meadow's flowers . . .

Even the white man, whose God walks and talks with him as friend to friend, cannot be exempt from the common destiny. We may be brothers after all: we shall see. One thing we know, which the white man may one day discover – our God is the same God. You may think now that you own Him as you wish to own our land, but you cannot. He is the God of man, and His compassion is equal for the red man and the white. This earth is precious to Him and to harm the earth is to heap contempt on its creator. The whites too shall pass; perhaps sooner than all other tribes. Continue to contaminate your bed, and you will one night suffocate in your own waste.'

(From a letter by Chief Seattle to the US President in 1855)

148

'For us God is above and beyond his creation. We aspire to reach God, but God and the world are not the same.

In the Hindu tradition the world is understood to be the dance of the god Shiva and the dance and the dancer cannot be separate. The world is not like a painting, a finished object which when complete is seen as separate from the painter. The universe is a living dance and God is in the heart of all beings and all things. We do not separate God and the world.

'I believe that the world is God's creation and therefore it is sacred. Human beings must act as responsible guardians and caring stewards. We must love the land and look after the earth in its glorious diversity. We have no right to plunder, pollute, exploit, destroy, kill or in any way disrespect God's creation. Like in a family God is the Father and we are His children and all members of the family should live in harmony with each other. God's family includes the animal and natural world. If we are sensitive and caring we can live with nature rather than against nature. The advance of science and technology requires that human beings live with greater sensitivity than ever before since we are now equipped with extremely powerful and potentially destructive tools. This destructive impulse is not part of God. God is good and good only.'
(Simon Phipps, Bishop of Lincoln, *Resurgence* November/December, 1986)

'For me the Divinity is neither good nor bad, it's like pure water and pure air. The human soul is also pure. Good and bad is a matter of perception. For example, from nature's point of view creeping buttercups or nettles are fine wherever they are, they will grow where the soil is right for them. From the human perspective a gardener struggles to remove the buttercups and nettles, hates them as weeds and complains when they overtake flowers. The rose and the thorn are part of the same plant, we cannot have one without the other. The mind always attempts to separate the good and evil, the decorative and the ugly, the useful and the non-useful, the weed and the flower. I have seen during my journey people pulling out foxgloves in one area and carefully planting them in another. If we are to live in harmony with God's family we need to love the wilderness, the weeds and the wet.'
(Satish Kumar, *Resurgence*, November/December, 1986)

FOR YOUR FOLDERS

► Explain why the Bishop of Lincoln believes the world to be sacred.
► Explain his views on science and technology.
► *'Every part of this earth is sacred to my people.'* After reading Chief Seattle's letter to the US President explain what he means.

► Why are the 'white man's' ideas strange to the Indians?
► Explain in your own words Chief Seattle's ideas about God.
► 'The whites too shall pass; perhaps sooner than all other tribes.' Comment on this statement.

FOR DISCUSSION

► Continue to contaminate your bed, and you will one night suffocate in your own waste.'

(Chief Seattle, 1855)

REFLECTIONS

'So God created man in His own image; in the image of God He created . . . them. God blessed them and said to them. "Be fruitful and increase, fill the earth and subdue it, rule over . . . every living thing that moves upon the earth." . . . So it was; and God saw all that He had made, and it was very good.'

(Genesis 1:27–29, 31)

'You appointed him ruler over everything you made; you placed him over all creation.'

(Psalm 8:6)

'A desacralized nature is in the power of humanity which is now able to destroy its own species and perhaps even all life on the earth. Our own technological inventions and our social processes are threatening to get the upper hand, to become as overpowering as nature once was. What needs to be emphasized today, therefore, is the way that God and His creation are "related" rather than their "separateness". The dignity of nature as creation needs to be bound up with our responsibility for the preservation of life.'

(The World Council of Churches)

POISONED AIR

'CUBATAO, near Sao Paulo, Brazil, is one of the most polluted industrial centres on earth. Its air contains twice the level of industrial particles considered lethal by the World Health Organization. Fish die in its polluted waters, trees turn to skeletons and more babies are born deformed here than anywhere else in Latin America. A 1982 industry report believed Brazil must "choose between pollution and recession".
Unfortunately, they've got both.
SUDBURY, in Ontario, Canada has the largest single source of artificial sulphur dioxide effluence in the world with its copper and nickel smelter. The annual output of 632,000 tonnes means that the nickel smelter has discharged more SO_2 between 1969 and 1979 than all the volcanoes in the history of the earth.

BRITAIN'S CENTRAL ELECTRICITY GENERATING BOARD is the largest single emitter of sulphur in Europe – its oil and coal-fired stations lacking any effective anti-pollutant controls. They are responsible for 2.6 million tons of sulphur, most of it blown away to fall on Scandinavia and Central Europe.

Our air and ground-water are fouled by the burning of fossil fuels in electricity generating stations, in cars, factories and homes. Sulphur dioxide and nitrogen oxide are released into the atmosphere to be washed back down in rain – with nasty consequences for the environment. And nuclear-powered energy is no alternative as the Chernobyl and Three Mile Island accidents have demonstrated. Ultimately we must use less energy to save our nature and ourselves.

TREE DAMAGE

Many forests in Europe and North America are dying from rain with the acidity of lemon juice. More than half West Germany's trees are affected.

FOOD LOSSES

Acidification of the soil means crop yields are reduced by 10–20% in Europe – an estimated loss of $500 million a year.

CRUMBLING SHRINES

Filthy air is threatening the world's most wonderful buildings: the Acropolis in Athens, St Paul's in London and Chartres cathedral are dissolving. Smoke from an oil refinery burn-off near the Taj Majal, India, is likely to turn the delicate marble of the Taj to gypsum within the next 50 years.

INCREASING FATALITIES

Millions suffer from smog in cities. More than 51,000 Americans died as a result of the polluted air in 1982, according to a US Congress Report. Cerebral lead poisoning threatens the children of traffic-clogged cities like Bangkok, Manila and Mexico City, where there is twice as much lead in gasoline as in the West.

RADIATION HAZARDS

Leaks from nuclear power plants endanger millions. Chernobyl, in April 1986, where a thermo-nuclear explosion blew off the roof of the reactor could cause anything between 5,000 and 50,000 cancer victims in Europe over the next 40 years. Further accidents in one of the world's 340 nuclear power plants are likely to happen once every decade. There have been two in the last seven years!'

(New Internationalist Publications)

Ozone fears as Amazon forest burns

THE amount of Amazon forest burnt down is estimated to have doubled in two years, leading to increased fears for the future of the ozone layer.

For the first time, Brazilian scientists have measured the exact amount of Amazon forest burnt down during the annual dry season to make way for cattle pasture and crops.

The numbers are terrifying. They found that in 1987 no less than 63,939 square miles went up in smoke. The total Amazon region covers over three million square miles.

About half the area burnt was virgin forest. What is more, the scientists have begun to investigate the possibility that the huge dense pall of smoke and gases released into the atmosphere

by the burning and then carried south by the regular wind currents could be contributing towards the thinning of the ozone layer in the Antarctic.

"The amount of smoke produced is so great that it's as though the Amazon had a hundred volcanos in eruption", said Dr Alberto Setzer the environmental engineer in charge of the forest fire monitoring project at Brazil's space research institute.

(Guardian, 18 April 1988)

FOR YOUR FOLDERS

▶ Design a poster called 'Creation in crisis' using some of the ideas from this unit.

▶ In the creation story in Genesis, human beings were given 'dominion' over nature. Find out what the word 'dominion' means and write a paragraph about the way that humanity has abused its gift of dominion.

▶ Explain what you think the statement by the World Council of Churches means.

▶ *'Inasmuch as you have done it unto one of the least of my brethren, you have down it unto me.'* (Matthew 25:40) Consider this teaching with regard to our treatment of the planet earth.

THINKING POINT

● **'The heart of a blue whale is the height of a tall man and weighs half a ton. Huge astonishing creatures of vast charm and mystery, whales are Grand Canyon and Mount Everest of the animal world. They are truly miraculous forms of life which have been the largest brained creatures on the planet for 30 times longer than humans have existed at all. Yet we, in our ignorance, continue to murder them.'**

(Heathcote Williams)

The universe is sacred

The Christian Church has not been blameless

In principle the Christian religion has taught that God created the earth and that human beings are the responsible stewards or managers of creation. Human beings should work wisely to protect what has been given to them, to work with nature and not against it. However, people have, and still do, exploit nature for greedy economic gain. Today, enormous multinational companies make vast sums of money by exploiting the earth's natural resources and usually show little concern for the environmental damage that they themselves cause.

Many people feel that some of the ideas in the Christian religion have been deliberately abused in the pursuit of power and wealth. They argue that our present environmental crisis has a lot to do with Christian arrogance. In particular they point to the idea that nature only exists to serve humanity, and that humanity as recorded in the Genesis account of creation has some sort of divine right to exploit nature. This has undoubtedly been true – the earth is there to be used and exploited – and the Churches have done very little to counter these destructive ideas. It has done little, either, to warn of the risks to the environment; nor to lead by example and show that a more simple life style is more in line with Jesus' teachings; nor to speak up and challenge the life styles of our consumer-ridden and wasteful, unaware society.

Often people have blamed science alone for the desperate crisis the earth now faces. To a certain extent this criticism is valid, but as 70 of the world's leading scientists wrote in 1983:

'We gave it away. We gave the power to people who didn't understand it and were not grown up enough or responsible enough to realize what they had.'

New messages

However, recently the Churches have begun to confront the crisis in creation. In this article, Ian Bradley outlines some of the changes in attitudes that are slowly influencing the Churches.

Is it nature or human nature?

'Christianity doesn't have a good Press in the Green movement and understandably so. The doctrine of man's dominion over the rest of creation, which is apparently spelled out in Genesis, has played a significant part in encouraging exploitative attitudes towards the world of nature in the West. However, slowly the Churches are beginning to look afresh at faith and practices to see if they can be given a greener tinge.

The World Council of Churches is engaged in a lot of work to develop a new "theology of nature" which will take a much more positive view of non-human creation. Several strong currents in contemporary Christianity are helping to create a much more positive attitude to the world of nature. Feminist theology is challenging long-dominant "macho" images of God and stressing instead the gentleness and fertility of the creation. The growing interest in both Eastern Orthodoxy and Celtic spirituality is leading to a more sacramental view of nature.

Traditionally both Catholics and Protestants have held to the idea that "nature is fallen". This has often been used to justify man's exploitation of the environment. Yet I believe that the doctrine of the fall of nature can help to provide a new "green" Christianity, which gives humans a key role in the redemption of the cosmos. Genesis says that God cursed the earth as a direct result of Adam's sin (Genesis 3). Responsibility for the fallen state of the world is thus laid at the door of humanity in a way that must strike a chord in an age when we are so conscious of the damage our species does to the environment. The Biblical idea of the Fall can be read as a parable of what happens when human beings seek to play God with the natural world.

There is another sense in which the doctrine of the Fall of nature can be interpreted to build a more ecological theology. Science has helped theologians move away from the idea of a once-and-for-all creation of a perfect world and to think in terms of a more open and uncompleted process. In this view, to talk of the natural world as being fallen is simply to stress its incompleteness and immaturity.

St Paul speaks of the whole creation "groaning in travail and waiting with eager longing for the sons of God". Instead of confronting God's non-human creation as something to be exploited for our own convenience, we stand together with it as fellow sufferers, equally the victims of frustration and imperfection, yet uniquely placed to redeem it through the exercise of love.'

(Adapted from *The Guardian*, 28 November 1988)

FOR YOUR FOLDERS

▶ Write an article explaining why many people believe that the Christian churches have not been blameless for our present environmental crisis.

▶ What examples of the Church looking 'afresh' at its beliefs and practices does Ian Bradley examine in his article?

▶ In what ways does he believe the 'Fall' can be interpreted so as to give Christianity a 'green tinge'?

! ▶ After reading the last three units on the present crisis facing planet earth, try to think how:

a the Churches;

b you as individuals; and

c governments

can try and avert a massive environmental catastrophe happening.

TALKING POINTS

● 'The universe is sacred. You cannot improve it. If you try and change it you will ruin it.'

(Tao Te Ching)

● 'Modern man . . . stands like a brutish infant, gloating over his meteoric rise to ascendancy, on the brink of a war to end all wars and effectively destroying this oasis of life in the solar system.'

(Greenpeace)

76 COURSEWORK

Coursework does not mean that you have to do an extra project on top of all your other school work. It will involve work that is done by you during the two years that you are doing this course. This work may take the form of classwork, homework, individual or group work.

Coursework usually means you submitting three 1000-word pieces of your own work; or, for some courses, in submitting one 3000-word piece of work.

In GCSE Religious Studies, there are three things that you need to consider for each piece of coursework. In unit 1 these were called three areas, and they are not difficult to understand. If you note these three areas, you could obtain a higher grade than you might imagine. In GCSE you are not competing against each other, instead the exam is intended to help you to improve your own skills and hence your own grades.

These three areas are called *knowledge, understanding* and *evaluation*. What do they mean?

Knowledge

You must show that you know the relevant facts related to the topic that you are studying. You must show that you are able to select the relevant facts, organize them and clearly present the facts and information.

Understanding

You must show that you understand this information. You can do this by:
- using information that is relevant;
- presenting the information to show that you understand the reasons behind any conclusion that is reached;
- presenting the information in such a way that shows that you understand the main ideas, issues and beliefs involved in the project, and understand their meaning and importance;
- showing that you are aware of the religious teachings involved in the topics, and wherever possible showing that you are able to *apply* these teachings to the various ideas in the project.

Evaluation

Evaluation means:
- being able to give *both sides* of an argument, an attitude or a belief;
- being able to *give your own ideas* and beliefs about something;
- being able to *show and give reasons* for the ideas that you are writing about.

Evaluation allows you to give your own views about something. It also enables you, if you wish, to talk about something that has happened to you, that may be relevant to the project.

These are the three areas; try to remember them. Sometimes they overlap – by knowing something, you understand it and by understanding something you can develop your own ideas about it.

Finding resources

Obviously, you will need to find information that is relevant to your project. Your teacher may be able to help but remember that this is *your own piece of work*. Ultimately it will be up to you to look for your own material. To a certain extent this book will help you, but it can't always give you *all* the relevant information. Here are some ideas for sources of information:
- school library and Religious Studies department;
- the local library;
- newspapers, magazines, television and radio;
- talking to parents, relatives and friends – discussing your topic with them. Things often become clearer if we talk about them;
- writing to organizations (see *Some important addresses*, p. 156). Remember to send a stamped addressed envelope;
- local churches and local ministers of religion;
- arranging for outside speakers to come into school.

Which topic?

The project must be related to the course that you are doing. Try to choose something that you find quite interesting – this will make it far more enjoyable and as a result will probably mean that you produce a better project. In this respect this book will help you – look through the contents page and browse through the book. Often something will catch your eye. Also, if something that is relevant comes up in the news, then this might help you. It is up to you which topic you do, just remember that it must be relevant to the course and interesting to you.

Always remember the three areas – knowledge, understanding and evaluation – to include these three keys is to ensure a successful project.

A good tip – when you start a project *ask questions*. Write these questions down. This method could help you to organize your project and give you a basic framework for your topic.

Example: Christian beliefs about God.

SOME QUESTIONS

- What do Christians think God is like?
- How do Christians try to define God?
- What do Christians say about God?
- Why do Christians believe in a God?
- What does the Bible teach about God?
- If there is a God why is there such suffering in the world? How do Christians answer this?
- What are your own views on the existence of God?

RESOURCES

- Books on famous Christians.
- The Bible.
- Organize an interview with somebody you know who believes in God.

THE THREE AREAS

- **Knowledge** – present information to show the main ideas about Christian belief in a God, drawing attention to the sorts of characteristics that Christians attribute to God.
- **Understanding** – explain the importance of belief in a God to Christians, and the ways that this belief affects Christian ideas and practices.
- **Evaluation** – consider and discuss issues like the problem of evil. Say what your own views are and give a reasoned personal view on the existence of a God.

Example: Apartheid.

SOME QUESTIONS

- What is racism?
- Why does racism exist (e.g. stereotyping, economic/political repression)?
- What does apartheid mean for the people of South Africa?
- What has been the response of the churches to apartheid (e.g. Dutch Reformed Church/Kairos Document)?
- How can a church like the Dutch Reformed Church support racist thinking?
- Why does apartheid raise questions of social ethics? What might these questions be?

RESOURCES

- Write to the Anti-Apartheid movement (see important addresses).
- Sections in this book.
- Newspapers/TV documentaries.

THE THREE AREAS

- **Knowledge** – present information to show the meaning and consequences of apartheid. Include details of the history of white domination in South Africa and the work of Church people like Huddleston, Tutu and Boesak.
- **Understanding** – explain what racism is, drawing attention to why it exists, what it means to the people of South Africa and how people/organizations respond to it.
- **Evaluation** – consider and discuss why you think apartheid is wrong. Say what you think can be done to abolish it and what the Churches in South Africa and Britain can do to help the situation. Consider other sorts of aparthied (i.e. systems of separation) in the world today and give your own view on the Churches' involvement in political struggles.

SOME IMPORTANT ADDRESSES

Action by Christians Against Torture
32 Wentworth Hills
Wembley, Middlesex HA9 9SG

African National Congress (ANC)
P O Box 38
28 Penton Street
London NW1 9PR

Amnesty International
5 Roberts Place
(off Bowling Green Lane)
London EC1R 0ED

Animal Aid
7 Castle Street
Tonbridge, Kent TN9 1BH

Anti-Apartheid Movement
13 Mandela Street
London NW1 0DW

Baptist Union
Baptist Church House
4 Southampton Row
London WC1B 4AB

Beat the Border
8 Cambray Place
Cheltenham
Gloucestershire GL50 1JS

British Council of Churches
2 Eaton Gate
London SW1W 9BL

Campaign Against the Arms Trade (CAAT)
11 Goodwin Street
London N4 3HO

Campaign for Nuclear Disarmament (CND)
22/24 Underwood Street
London N1 7JY

Catholic Agency for Overseas Development
(CAFOD)
21a Soho Square
London W1V 6NR

Catholic Housing Aid Society
189a Old Brompton Road
London SW5 0AR

Catholic Truth Society
38/40 Eccleston Square
London SW1P 1LT

Christian Aid
PO Box 1
London SW9 8BH

Christian Education Movement
2 Chester House
Pages Lane
London N10 1PR

Church of England Board for Social Responsibility
Church House
Dean's Yard
London SW1P 2N2

Church of England Children's Society
Old Town Hall
Kennington Road
London SE11

Commission for Racial Equality
10/12 Allington House
London SW1E 5EH

El Salvador Committee for Human Rights
83 Margaret Street
London W1N 7HB

European Christian Mission
50 Billing Road
Northampton NN1 5DH

Evangelical Alliance
19 Draycott Place
London SW3 2SG

Evangelical Christians for Racial Justice
12 Bell Barn Shopping Centre
Cregoe Street
Birmingham B15 2D2

Friends of the Earth (FOE)
26–28 Underwood Street
London N1 7JQ

Greenpeace
30–31 Islington Green
London N1 8XE

L'ARCHE
The Anchorage
25 Fairfield Crescent
Liverpool 6

L'ARCHE Lambeth
15 Norwood High Street
West Norwood
London SE27

Martin Luther King Memorial Trust
1/3 Hildreth Street
London SW12 9RQ

Methodist Church
1 Central Buildings
Westminster
London SW1

Minority Rights Group
29 Craven Street
London WC2N 5NT

Nicaraguan Solidarity Campaign
23 Beverden Street
London N1 6BH

Orthodox Church Information Service
64 Prebend Gardens
London W6 0XY

OXFAM
274 Banbury Road
Oxford OX2 7D2

Peace Pledge Union
Dick Sheppard House
6 Endsleigh Street
London WC1H 0DX

PAX Christi
St Francis of Assisi Centre
Pottery Lane
London W11 4NQ

Quakers ('The Religious Society of Friends')
Friends House
Euston Road
London NW1 2BJ

Salvation Army
101 Queen Victoria Street
London EC4 4EP

Samaritans
17 Uxbridge Road
Slough SL1 1SN

SHELTER
157 Waterloo Road
London SE1 8XF

Survival International Ltd
310 Edgware Road
London W2 1DY

Tear Fund
11 Station Road
Teddington
Middlesex TW11 9AA

United Nations Association
3 Whitehall Court
London SW1A 2EL

United Society for Propagation of the Gospel
15 Tufton Street
London SW1P 3QQ

World of Music and Dance (WOMAD)
Mill Lane
Box
Wilts SN14 9PN

World Vision
146 Queen Victoria Street
London EC4

As many of the organizations rely on donations, always send a stamped, self-addressed envelope.

For local organizations use your telephone directory or reference library.

GLOSSARY

Altar   table or raised level surface where the celebration of the Eucharist takes place

Amen   literally means 'may this be true' or 'so be it' – used to complete a prayer

Anglican   the name given to a member of the Church of England and to the Church of England itself

Apostle   literally 'one who is sent'. The name given to the eleven disciples of Jesus

Assumption   (the doctrine of) the belief that Mary ascended to heaven

Atonement   the belief that Jesus saved the world from its sin, through His death

Baptism   Christian rite of initiation

Bible   literally 'book', containing the sacred writings of Judaism and Christianity

Canon   a collection of books which have the authority of a religious community

Catechism   instruction by question and answer given to a person being prepared for Christian baptism

Charismatic Movement   a movement within Christianity that seeks the inspiration of the Holy Spirit in communal forms of worship

Church   1 the whole Christian community
2 a place where Christians meet for worship

Communion   literally means 'common sharing'

Confession   to admit a fault or one's sins.

Confirmation   rite of admisson into full membership of the Christian community

Consecration   an act whereby a building or person is set apart for sacred uses and responsibilities

Contemplation   the act of thinking deeply and quietly

Creed   a statement of belief.

Denominations   name given to the groups or Churches into which Christianity is divided

Disciple   literally 'one who learns' (see apostle)

Easter   Christian festival celebrating the rising of Jesus from death

Ecumenical   from Greek, a word meaning 'the whole inhabited world'

Eternal   everlasting

Fast   going without food, drink or certain foods as a religious observance

Festival   an enjoyable celebration (usually annually)

Grace   the loving help that Christians believe God gives to all human beings

Hymn   a religious poem set to music and sung during worship

Icon   a religious picture of a holy person

Immaculate Conception   usually refers to a belief that the Virgin Mary was born without sin

Incarnation   the belief that God appears on earth in human form

Infallible   literally 'without error'

Lent   a period of fasting before the Christian festival of Easter

Liturgy   a form or order of public worship

Martyr   someone who is put to death for remaining loyal to a belief

Mass   word used by some Christians to describe the Eucharist

Pater Noster   the Latin words for 'Our Father'. It refers to the Lord's Prayer, which begins with these words

Priest   person authorized to officiate at religious ceremonies, members of the Roman Catholic and Anglican Churches ordained and authorized to give the sacraments

Redemption   to obtain freedom from sin and evil

Repentance   sorrow for sins, and the determination to try to do better

Sacrament   an outward, visible sign of an inward, invisible spiritual blessing obtained through certain rites

Transcendent   a reality that is above and beyond this world

Transubstantiation   a belief that the bread and wine during the Eucharist mysteriously become the actual body and blood of Christ

Trinity   the Christian doctrine that there is one God in three persons. Father, Son and Holy Spirit

Vocation   a special call from, or choosing by God to do certain types of work and service

Word (the)   to Christians this refers to Jesus Christ

INDEX